Robert
Louis
Stevenson

Robert Louis Stevenson

Finding Treasure Island

Angelica Shirley Carpenter & Jean Shirley

Lerner Publications Company • Minneapolis

To Jane

Text permissions acknowledgments and source notes appear on pages 134–138, which are an extension of the copyright page.

Copyright © 1997 by Angelica Shirley Carpenter and Jean Shirley

Library of Congress Cataloging-in-Publication Data

Carpenter, Angelica Shirley.
    Robert Louis Stevenson : finding Treasure Island / Angelica
Shirley Carpenter and Jean Shirley
        p. cm.
    Includes bibliographical references (p.) and index.
    Summary: Describes the life of the man who wrote "Kidnapped,"
"Treasure Island," and "A Child's Garden of Verses."
    ISBN 0-8225-4955-7 (alk. paper)
    1. Stevenson, Robert Louis, 1850–1894—Biography—Juvenile
literature. 2. Authors, Scottish—19th century—Biography—Juvenile
literature. [1. Stevenson, Robert Louis, 1850–1894. 2. Authors,
Scottish.] I. Shirley, Jean. II. Title.
PR5493.C29 1997
828'.809—dc21
    [B]   96–48274

Manufactured in the United States of America
1 2 3 4 5 6 – JR – 02 01 00 99 98 97

Contents

Preface

Robert Louis Stevenson wrote: "I like biography far better than fiction myself; fiction is too free. In biography you have your little handful of facts, little bits of a puzzle, and you sit and think and fit 'em together this way and that."

Thanks to all the authors who have written about RLS, providing us with bits of the puzzle. Special thanks to Robin Hill, Alan Marchbank, Bernadette Plissari, and Jim Winegar for a warm welcome into the Robert Louis Stevenson club.

In our book, for brevity's sake, we called RLS "Lewis" or "Louis" and used first names for his immediate family. We called Fanny Sitwell "Mrs. Sitwell," as she is always referred to in that way.

After his grandfather Balfour died, Robert Louis Stevenson wrote: "He moves in my blood and whispers words to me, and sits efficient in the very knot and center of my being." My mother and co-author Jean Shirley died as we finished this manuscript, but like Louis's grandfather, she is still with me, especially in this book.

Angelica Shirley Carpenter

MARSHALL
•ISLANDS

BUTARITARI–

GILBERT
ISLANDS

APEMAMA

AUSTRALIA

Sydney

Auckland

NEW
ZEALAND

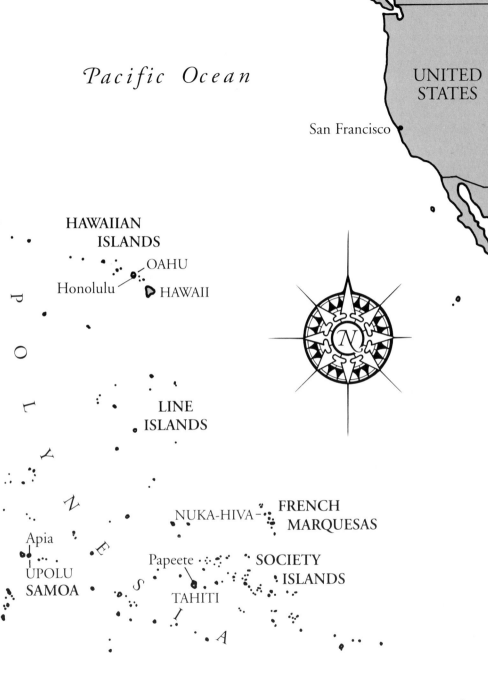

Pacific Ocean

UNITED
STATES

San Francisco

HAWAIIAN
ISLANDS

OAHU

Honolulu

HAWAII

P
O
L
Y
N
E
S
I
A

LINE
ISLANDS

NUKA-HIVA

FRENCH
MARQUESAS

Apia

Papeete

SOCIETY
ISLANDS

UPOLU
SAMOA

TAHITI

Robert Louis Stevenson's
Sojourns in the South Pacific

"Where should we adventure, to-day that we're afloat?" wrote
Robert Louis Stevenson (right) *in* A Child's Garden of Verses.
Here he spots land while sailing in the South Seas.

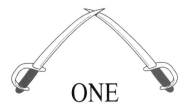

ONE

The Land of Counterpane

1850–1860

*I*n 1888 author Robert Louis Stevenson traveled halfway around the world to explore the islands of the South Pacific. Sailing from San Francisco in a luxurious, ninety-five-foot yacht, he traveled with his wife, mother, and stepson, their maid, and a ship's crew of five.

After thirty days at sea, they reached the islands known then as the French Marquesas. "Land!" came the cry, just at dawn, and the sleeping passengers woke instantly. Tumbling into their dressing gowns, they rushed on deck.

As the sun rose, volcanic islands came into view. "Like the pinnacles of some ornate and monstrous church, they stood there," Louis said, "in the sparkling brightness of the morning, the fit signboard of a world of wonders." What would they find, he wondered, on the island of Nuka-hiva? Some called it the man-eating island, though cannibalism had been outlawed there for two years. He watched Nuka-hiva's lofty mountains, "no more than a grey haze at first, gradually growing distinct as we drew nearer and nearer, till at last the

9

green masses of foliage, the beach, and the curving bay came into sight."

Soon they smelled land smells—wild lime and vanilla—and heard sheep bleating from the hills. Then a village came into view, and people gathering on the beach. Louis wrote: "Before yet the anchor plunged a canoe was already paddling from the hamlet. It contained two men: one white, one brown and tattooed across the face with bands of blue, both in immaculate white European clothes: the resident trader, Mr. Regler, and the native chief, Taipi-Kikino. 'Captain, is it permitted to come on board?' were the first words we heard among the islands. Canoe followed canoe till the ship swarmed with stalwart, six-foot men in every state of undress; some in a shirt, some in a loin-cloth, one in a handkerchief imperfectly adjusted."

So began Louis's greatest adventure. Ten months later, he wrote: "By the time I am done with this cruise I shall have the material for a very singular book of travels: names of strange stories and characters, cannibals, pirates, ancient legends, old Polynesian poetry."

More than one hundred years after his death, Robert Louis Stevenson remains one of the world's most famous authors. His books—*Treasure Island, Kidnapped, The Strange Case of Dr. Jekyll and Mr. Hyde,* and *A Child's Garden of Verses*—are still bestsellers.

Robert Louis Stevenson was born on November 13, 1850, in a small stone house at 8 Howard Place in Edinburgh, the capital city of Scotland. His parents named him Robert Lewis Balfour Stevenson for both grandfathers: Robert Stevenson, an engineer, and Lewis Balfour, a Presbyterian minister. They called him Lewis, or Lew.

Lewis's parents had met on a train—Thomas, the serious young civil engineer, drawn to warm-hearted Maggie Balfour, "the minister's white-haired lassie."

Thomas's family, "the lighthouse Stevensons," owned a civil engineering firm that had built all the lighthouses in Scotland and more lighthouses, railways, and bridges around the world. Thomas and Maggie expected young Lewis to join his father and uncles in the family firm someday and to become a leader in the Presbyterian Church.

Blond and handsome like his mother, Lewis was a plump, healthy baby. Maggie adored him and played with him as if

Maggie with Lewis at age four. In the 1850s, upper-class boys wore dresses and long curls.

she were a child herself. Thomas, usually strict and somber, unbent to entertain his son. He nicknamed Lew "Smout," the Scots term for young salmon.

Deeply in love, Thomas and Maggie had every advantage except good health. Thomas suffered from bronchitis, Maggie from lingering colds. She stayed in bed each day until noon, while servants cared for Lewis. Her self-pampering may have been justified: in those days, before antibiotics, people died easily, especially during harsh winters.

When Lewis was eighteen months old, the Stevensons moved to a larger house at No. 1 Inverleith Terrace. About this same time, they hired a nurse—a strong, healthy woman named Alison Cunningham. "Cummy," as Lewis called her, was a fisherman's daughter and an experienced baby nurse at twenty-nine years old. Lively and dramatic, she entertained the toddler with stories and songs.

At age two, Lewis caught the croup, and he could not seem to recover. Almost overnight "the round, fair-haired baby turned scrawny, bug-eyed, pigeon breasted, with a jangled nervous system and a genius for running fevers." For the rest of his childhood, Lewis suffered from colds, chest problems, and contagious diseases.

Sick or well, he was the heart of the household, and Maggie recorded his activities in her diary. He liked to play church, she reported, and once drew a picture, asking her, "Mama, I have drawed a man's body; shall I draw his soul now?"

At age six, Lewis entered a contest with his cousins. Their uncle promised a prize of one pound sterling for the best "History of Moses." Lewis, who had not yet learned to write, won with a story dictated to Maggie. "From that time forward," reported his mother, "it was the desire of his heart to be an author."

Cummy was "more patient than I can suppose of an angel," Lewis said.

Even after he learned to write, Lew dictated stories to Maggie and Cummy, and they read to him and told him stories. In those days, few books had been written especially for children. When Maggie read Shakespeare's play *Macbeth* to her young son, Lewis said it made "newts and snakes and others to crawl up and down my spine." Cummy scared Lewis, too, with stories about the devil, who took bad boys to hell, and about the Covenanters, who had lived in Scotland in a period so bloody it was known as the killing time.

Just as American children were told stories of the Wild West, Scottish children heard tales of the Covenanters, who had lived in the 1600s. Their name came from a document known as the National Covenant. It was signed by Scots in protest when King Charles I tried to replace the Scottish prayer book with that of the Church of England. After many battles, the Covenanters won the right to keep their Presbyterian prayer service.

Two centuries after the Covenanters, when Lew was a child, Covenanter tales were part of Scottish folklore. Cummy told stories dramatically, in an old-fashioned Scottish accent that Lewis admired. He imitated her way of talking and using her hands for emphasis.

Starting school at the age of six, Lewis quickly became "the butt of the school from the oddity of his appearance"— thin and frail, almost skeletal. Cummy walked him to school, and if his shoes got wet, she "changed his feet," amusing his classmates.

On Saturdays, bundled against the cold, Lewis and Cummy set out to read cheap weekly newspapers known as "penny dreadfuls." At the stationer's shop they pored over the latest installments of illustrated adventures like "The Discovery of the Dead Body in the Blue Marl Pit" and "The Baronet Unmasked." Lew claimed that he had learned to read by studying these stories. Sometimes they walked to the harbor to see ships, or to Warriston Cemetery, where Cummy told stories of "resurrection-men," who dug up dead bodies.

Cummy taught Lewis her religious beliefs, which were stricter than his parents'. She disapproved of dancing, playing cards, reading novels, and going to the theater—even though the Stevensons sometimes did those things. Lewis amused Thomas and Maggie by lecturing them on their misdeeds.

Greyfriars Kirkyard in Edinburgh, where Scots signed the National Covenant in 1638, starting a bloody civil war. This is how the churchyard looked during Lewis's lifetime.

To entertain Lewis, Thomas carried on silly conversations with imaginary people.

Unusual parents for the time, they allowed their only child to speak freely on any subject. Imitating them, Lewis developed elegant manners and "owlish, grown-uppish talk" that set him apart from his schoolmates. But the sophisticated boy could change instantly into a spoiled tyrant. Impatient and demanding, Lew cried easily when thwarted, and found little difficulty getting his own way.

His happiest days were spent with his cousins at their grandfather Lewis Balfour's manse—a minister's house—in Colinton, a village four miles southwest of Edinburgh. Built on the banks of the River Leith, the manse was a place like no other, Lewis said, with "the garden cut into provinces by a great hedge of beech . . . the smell of water rising from all round, with an added tang of paper-mills; the sound of water everywhere . . . the birds on every bush and from every corner of the overhanging woods pealing out their notes until the air throbbed with them."

Lewis's grandfather was white-haired, imposing, and stern. Though the old man frightened his grandson, Lewis loved the way he talked and preached, with an old-fashioned, broad Scottish accent.

Aunt Jane, Maggie's sister, who ran the Colinton household, spoiled her nieces and nephews. She bought them toy soldiers and comforted those who were homesick—some cousins had come all the way from India.

Lewis led his cousins in games, inventing scary adventures on a dark pathway that led from the garden to the kirkyard, or churchyard. There, Lewis said, "the tombstones were thick, and after nightfall 'spunkies' [ghosts] might be seen to dance, at least by children."

Lewis had fifty first cousins; Bob Stevenson, his favorite and best friend, was three years older than Lewis. When Lewis was six, Bob spent the winter at Inverleith Terrace.

That spring the Stevensons moved again, to No. 17 Heriot Row in New Town, a more elegant section of Edinburgh. Lewis's third-floor nursery overlooked the Queen Street Gardens. Though the room faced south, it was still cold and damp.

Lewis's winters were isolated. He spent many hours sick

in bed, covered up with his counterpane, or bedspread. Years later he wrote "The Land of Counterpane."

> When I was sick and lay a-bed,
> I had two pillows at my head,
> And all my toys beside me lay
> To keep me happy all the day.
>
> And sometimes for an hour or so
> I watched my leaden soldiers go,
> With different uniforms and drills,
> Among the bed-clothes, through the hills;
>
> And sometimes sent my ships in fleets
> All up and down among the sheets;
> Or brought my trees and houses out,
> And planted cities all about.
>
> I was the giant great and still
> That sits upon the pillow-hill,
> And sees before him, dale and plain,
> The pleasant land of counterpane.

Sometimes Lewis was too ill to play. Often he awoke in terror from a nightmare: the devil was coming to take him away! Afraid he would die if he fell asleep, Lewis struggled to stay awake.

Thomas comforted Lewis by telling him stories of ships, old sailors, stagecoaches, and robbers—stories from his own childhood. When Thomas went to bed, Lew's fears returned. "I remember repeatedly . . . waking from a dream of Hell," he said, "clinging to . . . the bed, with my knees and chin together, my soul shaken, my body convulsed with agony."

Then, Cummy to the rescue! "How well I remember her lifting me out of bed, carrying me to the window, and showing me one or two lit windows up in Queen Street across the

*No. 17 Heriot Row faces Queen Street Gardens, where Lewis
pretended to be a pirate.*

dark belt of gardens; where also, we told each other, there
might be sick little boys and their nurses waiting, like us, for
the morning." A grown-up Lewis realized that Cummy had
frightened him unnecessarily with scary stories and talk of
the devil, but he loved her all his life.

"I have three powerful impressions of my childhood:" he
wrote, "my sufferings when I was sick, my delights in conva-
lescence at my grandfather's manse . . . and the unnatural ac-
tivity of my mind after I was in bed at night."

Swanston, the Stevensons' summer home, overlooked the Pentland Hills. Lewis wrote about the "hills of home" in his pamphlet "The Pentland Rising" and in the novel St. Ives.

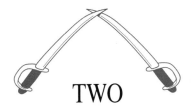

TWO

The Hills of Home

1861–1866

$\mathcal{T}$ap, tap, tap! At age eleven, Lewis played tricks on the neighbors, knocking on their windows after dark, then running away. Healthier than before, he had learned to ride horseback and often galloped recklessly across the countryside with his cousin Bob.

After Lewis's grandfather Balfour died in 1860, Lewis spent summers traveling with Maggie and Thomas. Traveling by train made it easy to explore Scotland. Wherever they went, Lewis walked for miles around the countryside, and he learned to enjoy canoeing and swimming.

Each fall his parents enrolled him in school, but whether he was at day school or boarding school, Lewis never stayed long. He left to travel with Thomas and Maggie, or because he was ill or too unhappy to stay. He preferred to study alone, with a tutor. Although he was good at mathematics, Lewis never learned to spell well, even when he became a best-selling author. Languages were his best subjects: Greek, Latin, German, and especially French.

At home and at school, Lewis produced magazines of horror stories and South Sea adventures. In one continuing story, he ended an episode with the heroes shipwrecked in India, sentenced to be burned alive.

Parties pleased Lewis, who liked to dress up. Admiring mothers called him "the little Frenchman" for his elegant clothes, sophisticated manners, and the way he talked with his hands.

In 1863, Maggie's doctor prescribed a winter stay on the French Riviera. Lewis accompanied her to Menton, France, with Cummy. Cummy had become Maggie's maid, as twelve-year-old Lew was too old for a nanny.

Cummy, who distrusted Catholics, was horrified by French religious customs. She disapproved of holy water, incense, and religious processions where marchers wore false faces and carried statues of saints. "Wickedness unchecked," she termed these practices. Each day she found something new to criticize.

At first Lewis was shocked, too, but soon he noticed that the French seemed happy, despite Cummy's disapproval. He loved the warm weather, relaxed vacation living, and the French language, which he learned to speak fluently.

Lew's cousin Bessie Stevenson traveled with them. She thought that "in some ways, [Lewis] was more like a boy of sixteen. [Thomas] had a great belief (inherited from his father) in the educational value of travel, and to this end and for the benefit of [Lewis] he devoted his whole energies in the five months abroad. In the hotel at Nice he began to take [Lewis] to the smoking-room with him; there my uncle was always surrounded by a group of eager and amused listeners—English, American, and Russian—and every subject, political, artistic, and theological, was discussed and argued."

Sometimes Lewis dined with strangers at the hotel's *table d'hôte,* a common table for guests, and held up his end of the conversation in several languages. The Stevensons returned to France each winter.

In 1863, Thomas took Lewis on a tour of lighthouses to introduce him to the family business. Arguing amiably, they took long walks to places Lew knew from Covenanter tales, stopping to pet dogs or to chat with children along the way.

At home or abroad, Thomas thought like an engineer. Lewis wrote: "My father would pass hours on the beach, brooding over the waves, counting them, noting their least deflection, noting when they broke . . . to me, at the time, extremely wearisome. . . . The river was to me a pretty and various spectacle; I could not see—I could not be made to see—it otherwise. To my father it was a chequerboard of lively forces. . . . [My father said] 'suppose you were to blast that boulder, what would happen? Follow it—use the eyes that God has given you: can you not see that a great deal of land would be reclaimed upon this side?' It was to me like school in holidays; but to him . . . a delight."

Lewis felt proud of his father. Thomas, experimenting with optics, had perfected the revolving light for lighthouses. Lewis wrote, "Whenever I smell salt water, I know I am not far from one of the works of my ancestors. The Bell Rock [a lighthouse] stands monument for my grandfather; the Skerry Vhor for my Uncle Alan; and when the lights come out at sundown along the shores of Scotland, I am proud to think they burn more brightly for the genius of my father."

But Lewis wanted to be a writer, not an engineer. At home or abroad, he observed people and language. He invented dialogues, playing all the parts and later writing them down. He eavesdropped, too, and said, "I kept always two books in my pocket, one to read, one to write in . . . and often exercised myself in writing down conversations from memory."

Reading widely in several languages, he absorbed poetry, history, and fiction: Covenanter tales, *Robinson Crusoe, The Arabian Nights,* Alexandre Dumas, Scottish classics, Shakespeare, and American authors. Lewis practiced writing in the style of different authors to understand what made their writing good. As a young man, he was thrilled to meet R. M. Ballantyne, one of his favorite writers, whose book *The Coral Island* was a boys' adventure tale set in the South Seas.

At his father's urging, Lewis wrote the history of a Covenanter battle. Thomas liked it so well that he had one hundred copies printed. The pamphlet, "The Pentland Rising," was Lewis's first published work.

In 1867, when Lewis was sixteen, the Stevensons rented Swanston Cottage, five miles south of Edinburgh in the Pentland Hills. Summer after summer for fourteen years, they returned to that beautiful setting, described by Lewis: "Upon the main slope of the Pentlands . . . a bouquet of old trees stands round a white farmhouse; and from a neighbouring dell you can see smoke rising and leaves rustling in the breeze. Straight above, the hills climb a thousand feet in the air. The neighbourhood, about the time of lambs, is clamorous with the bleating of flocks; and you will be awakened in the grey of early summer mornings by the barking of a dog, or the voice of a shepherd shouting to the echoes."

As he hiked through the hills, talking to farmers and shepherds, Lewis learned the local accent, which became his version of Scots. A ploughman told how Lew would "go up wi' me when I was ploughin'—but he'd never go far without taking out his pencil and notebook to get something down I'd said."

Engineering, Lewis said of his father's profession, "takes a man into the open air . . . it carries him to wild islands; it gives him a taste of the genial dangers of the sea."

Louis at sixteen in his black velvet jacket. With friends he formed the L.J.R. society—Liberty, Justice, and Reverence—vowing to "disregard everything our parents have taught us."

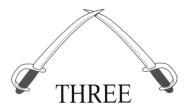

THREE

Velvet Coat

1866–1873

*I*n the late 1860s, an exotic figure walked the streets of Edinburgh: a tall young man with a springy step and a thin, stooped profile, like a question mark. His cloak swirled behind him in the wind, and so did his long fair hair. At this time, long hair and cloaks were seldom seen. Lewis also wore a velvet jacket (wool was customary), soft-collared shirt (stiff collars were fashionable), and a sailor's neckerchief instead of a necktie. His favorite soft, low-crowned hat, called a wideawake, made children laugh aloud. "As for his clothes, of which a great deal has been said," wrote Lew's cousin Graham Balfour, "he dressed to please himself."

While a student at the University of Edinburgh, Lewis changed his name from Robert Lewis Balfour Stevenson to Robert Louis Stevenson. Though he changed Lewis to Louis, he still used the same pronunciation, and his family called him Louis or Lou.

Each morning Louis, who still lived at home, ate breakfast with his parents in New Town. Then he walked up the hill

Louis called Edinburgh a "quaint, grey, castled city, where the bells clash of a Sunday, and the wind squalls, and the salt showers fly and beat."

past Edinburgh Castle, to the university in the medieval Old Town. At university, according to Lou, "All classes rub shoulders on the greasy benches [in the classrooms]. The raffish young gentleman in gloves must measure his scholarship with the plain, clownish laddie from the parish school."

Often the raffish young Lou found no time for school. Instead he explored the roughest neighborhoods of Edinburgh. "I was the companion of seamen, chimney-sweeps, and thieves," wrote Louis. "My circle was being continually changed by the action of the police magistrate." He spent his allowance in pubs and brothels, becoming popular with prostitutes, who nicknamed him "Velvet Coat."

Knowing poor people gave Louis a taste for social justice. He became a "red-hot Socialist," defending beggars and prostitutes and criticizing New Town society for its double standards. In New Town, civic leaders set strict rules for proper behavior, but some of the same men sneaked off to brothels and bars.

Though New Town society tolerated Lou good-naturedly, Thomas and Maggie worried about their son. They invited his respectable friends to dinner: Walter Simpson, whose famous doctor father had discovered chloroform, and Charles Baxter, a lawyer's son.

Though he often skipped classes, somehow Louis learned enough engineering to help Thomas during summer vacations. On a job at Anstruther Harbour, Louis, who looked young for his age, enjoyed hearing it said of him, "That's the man that's in charge." At another job, in Wick, he descended underwater in a diving suit to help rescue a worker.

Louis worked hard at his writing, which he sometimes showed to fellow students. He said, "they had the friendliness to be quite plain with me. 'Padding,' said one. Another wrote: 'I cannot understand why you do lyrics so badly.' No more could I!"

In 1869, Louis was elected to the Speculative Society, a snobbish, male literary and debating club. Wearing full evening dress, the thirty members met in candlelit, smoke-filled rooms once a week. At the Spec, Louis helped found *Edinburgh University Magazine.*

His best friend was still his cousin Bob Stevenson. In 1870, Bob returned to Edinburgh after graduating from Cambridge University. An artist whose paintings did not sell, Bob lived modestly on a small inheritance. The tall, charming, eccentric young man helped introduce a new slang term to Edinburgh: bohemian.

Bohemians—Bob considered himself one, and soon, so did Louis—were artists and intellectuals who challenged conventional morality. Scorning established manners and beliefs, most lived frugally. Most, like Bob and Louis, had no other choice.

Bob "taught Louis to drink and think," said one friend, and Louis wrote, "The mere return of Bob changed at once and for ever the course of my life; I can give you an idea of my relief only by saying that I was at last able to breathe." To Bob and Louis, art—including writing—was all-important; their elders were dull hypocrites, and New Town society was a joke.

In April 1871, on a walk with his father, Louis found the courage to tell Thomas that he could not become an engineer. Louis's cousin Etta, who was visiting Heriot Row, wrote: "This [news] was a great blow and terrible disappointment to dear Uncle Tom, as for generations the Stevensons had all been very clever civil engineers. . . . And Uncle Tom was more disappointed still when Lou declared that he wanted to go in for a literary life, as Uncle Tom thought he would make nothing at that—in fact that it was just a sort of excuse for leading a lazy life!" Father and son struck a bargain: if Louis would study law, and if he could pass the bar examination, Thomas would give him a thousand pounds sterling and would let him try a career as a writer.

At Edinburgh University, Louis performed in amateur theatricals. A poor actor, he took small parts and enjoyed dressing up.

Continuing to write, Louis studied law and worried about another personal problem: he had begun to question his religious faith. For months he agonized over his lack of belief and the fact that he had to hide his feelings from his parents. In February 1873, he wrote to his friend Charles Baxter:

> MY DEAR BAXTER,—The thunderbolt has fallen with a vengeance now. On Friday night . . . my father put [to] me one or two questions as to beliefs, which I candidly answered. I really hate all lying so much now . . . but if I had foreseen the real hell of everything since, I think I should have lied, as I have done so often before. . . . I think I could almost find it in my heart to retract, but it is too late; and again, am I to live my whole life as one falsehood? . . . I reserve (as I told them) many points until I acquire fuller information, and do not think I am thus justly to be called "horrible atheist." . . . O, Lord, what a pleasant thing it is to have just damned the happiness of (probably) the only two people who care a damn about you in the world!

When she heard Louis's response to his father's questions, Maggie told him, "This is the heaviest affliction that has ever befallen me."

Thomas was furious. "I have worked for you and gone out of my way for you," he said, "and the end of it is that I find you in opposition to the Lord Jesus Christ. . . . I would ten times sooner see you lying in your grave than that you should be shaking the faith of other young men and bringing ruin on other houses as you have brought it upon this."

Though Thomas could not bring himself to disown Louis, their happy companionship was ruined. Thomas searched religious books for arguments to save his son's soul. Tired of the conflict, Louis wrote to Baxter, "A little absence is the only chance."

Thomas agreed, sending Louis to Suffolk, England, to visit his cousin Maud, a childhood playmate from Colinton. She lived with her husband, the Reverend Thomas Babington, in a gracious Georgian rectory with a large garden and a moat.

A house guest, Fanny Sitwell, recalled Louis's arrival. "I saw a slim youth in a black velvet jacket and straw hat," she wrote, "with a knapsack on his back, walking up the avenue."

Louis saw a petite, dark-haired woman, a famous beauty who was separated from her husband, a clergyman. At thirty-four, she was twelve years older than Louis. She supported herself and her young son Bertie with translations. Separation was shocking in those days, and so was Mrs. Sitwell's close friendship with Sidney Colvin, a well-known author and critic.

Mrs. Sitwell wrote to Colvin, urging him to come meet the charming young writer. She and Louis quickly became friends. Sitting together under the trees, his head on her knee, her hand stroking his long hair, Louis fell in love.

Sidney Colvin liked Louis, too. He introduced Louis in literary circles and helped him to get published. Though Louis deferred always to Colvin as Mrs. Sitwell's "official" admirer, he tried to win her for himself. Being in love gave Louis self-confidence. After he returned home, he wrote Mrs. Sitwell long letters. A cousin, he reported, had told Thomas that Bob was responsible for Louis's lack of faith. Thomas, relieved to have someone else to blame for his son's downfall, grew calmer, and he and Lou resumed their walks.

To hold up his part of the bargain with his father, Louis resigned himself to studying law. He fell ill, losing weight from his thin frame. He could not sleep, and his face twitched constantly with a nervous tic. A famous doctor diagnosed acute nerve exhaustion and, knowing Louis's problems with his parents, prescribed a stay alone on the French Riviera.

The frontispiece to Louis's first published book showed Pan, the
Greek god of pastures, flocks, and shepherds, and Louis and
Walter Simpson paddling their canoes.

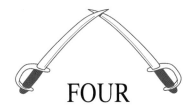

FOUR

Ordered South

1873–1876

$\mathcal{L}$ouis returned to the resort town of Menton, France. In a letter to Mrs. Sitwell, he described his arrival at the train station: "I gave up my baggage to an hotel porter and set off to walk at once. I was somewhat confused as yet to my directions. . . . Suddenly, as I was going forward . . . I was met by a great volley of odours out of the lemon and orange gardens, and the past linked on to the present, and in a moment, in the twinkling of an eye, the whole scene fell before me into order, and I was at home."

Bordered by sea and mountains, Menton was especially popular with the British. It was a treatment center for patients suffering from tuberculosis, or consumption, as it was called then. In Louis's lifetime there was no cure for this fatal disease, but some patients improved with rest and a stay by the sea.

Louis took a room in a British boarding house. Emaciated and exhausted, he stayed in bed, so ill that he lost his ability to speak French. As time passed, he began to notice his surroundings: flowers, work crews of flower-gatherers from the perfume industry, and moonrise over the Italian coast—a mile away. Louis wrote a declaration of independence to his father, knowing it might mean "ultimate rupture."

Thomas replied by telegram: "Quite satisfied with your letter—keep your mind easy." Later Louis learned that his parents thought he was out of his mind and should be humored.

In December 1873, Louis's essay "Roads," about his experiences in Suffolk, appeared in the *Portfolio Magazine,* and Sidney Colvin, who had helped to get it published, came to Menton. The two young men spent sunny afternoons in olive groves or floating on boats, talking and reading aloud.

Soon Louis's ability to speak French returned, and he and Colvin, who also spoke the language, moved to a French hotel. There Louis encountered two Russian sisters, both older than he was, both beautiful, charming, and married.

Princess Zassetsky, mother of ten, author of Russian comedies, flirted with Louis, and so did her sister Madame Garschine. The women spoke openly of their private lives, and Louis wrote to Mrs. Sitwell: "They do what they want with a perfect frankness."

Louis wrote an essay, "Ordered South," about his trip to France. Published in *Macmillan's Magazine,* it was his first writing to attract critical attention.

In April 1874, Louis visited his cousin Bob Stevenson at Bob's home in Paris. Though the city was still being rebuilt after civil war in 1871, Louis was drawn to its beauty and its sophisticated bohemian society. Artists and intellectuals welcomed the witty young writer. Some even dressed as eccentrically as he did.

Reluctantly, Louis returned to Edinburgh, where Thomas raised his allowance to seven pounds a month. Now Louis had a study at Heriot Row, in addition to his bedroom. Working for a law firm, he wrote in his spare time, publishing essays and short stories, earning modest fees that helped him travel.

In 1875, Louis met William Ernest Henley, a poet. Henley had come to Edinburgh to see the famous Dr. Joseph Lister, and Lister had amputated Henley's foot to stop tuberculosis of the bone. Now Henley's other foot was threatened.

A friend took Louis to visit Henley in his hospital room. Louis wrote: "It was very sad to see him there . . . the poor fellow sat up in his bed with his hair and beard all tangled and talked as cheerfully as if he had been in a King's palace." After Henley's foot was saved, he moved to London, where a visiting Louis introduced him to literary friends.

In June 1875, a visitor from New Zealand came to Heriot Row. Louis wrote to Mrs. Sitwell, "Awfully nice man here tonight. Public servant—New Zealand. Telling us all about the South Sea Islands till I was sick with desire to go there: beautiful places, green forever; perfect climate; perfect shapes of men and women, with red flowers in their hair; and nothing to do but to study oratory and etiquette, sit in the sun, and pick up the fruits as they fall. Navigator's Island [Samoa] is the place; absolute balm for the weary."

In July 1875, Lou passed the Scottish bar examination. His cousin Etta Younger wrote: "I remember the afternoon in which we drove into town from Swanston to hear the result of the examination. The excitement and joy was tremendous when he heard that he had passed. . . . We were driving in the big, open barouche, and nothing would satisfy Lou but that he would sit on the top of the carriage, that was thrown back open, with his feet on the seat, between his mother and father, where they were sitting; and he kept waving his hat and calling out to people he passed, whether known or unknown, just like a man gone mad."

True to his promise, Thomas gave Louis one thousand pounds sterling, which Louis used for a canoe trip with his friend Walter Simpson. They traveled from Belgium to France. Canoes were seldom seen on the continent, and these canoes were remarkable: each had a sail and a small British flag, the Union Jack. Lou's boat was the *Arethusa,* named after a nymph in Greek mythology; Simpson's, the *Cigarette.* "We made quite a stir in *Antwerp Docks,*" wrote Louis. The boats and his traveling costume attracted a crowd of cheering Belgian children. "They could not make enough of my red sash;" reported Louis, "and my knife filled them with awe."

The weather was cold and wet, but they carried dry clothes in india-rubber bags and slept in boarding houses and inns. Some places would not admit them. "Out with you—out of the door!" screeched one landlady, as Louis tried to explain why they looked so scruffy. *"Sortez! sortez! sortez par la porte!"* Louis's humorous account of their journey, and of the people they met, became his first published book, *An Inland Voyage.*

Louis and Simpson ended their trip in the Forest of Fontainebleau, forty miles southeast of Paris. Here a string of picturesque villages attracted artists, students, and models—and Bob Stevenson awaited them.

On July 1, 1876, Louis arrived at the Hôtel Chevillon in Grez-sur-Loing, just as the guests finished dinner. There he saw two women, Fanny Osbourne, petite and dark-haired, with her eighteen-year-old daughter Belle. Fanny's eight-year-old son Lloyd was also present.

Later Lloyd described Louis's entrance: "Then in the dusk of a summer's day, as we all sat at dinner about the long *table d'hôte* . . . there was a startling sound at one of the open windows giving on the street, and in vaulted a young man

Because Fanny Osbourne had come to Europe from California, Louis nicknamed her "The Wild Woman of the West."

with a dusty knapsack on his back. . . . He was tall, straight, and well-formed, with a fine ruddy complexion, clustering light-brown hair, a small tawny mustache, and extraordinarily brilliant brown eyes. . . . I gazed at him in spell-bound admiration."

Fanny in the riverside garden of the Hôtel Chevillon with Louis's cousin Bob (wearing striped socks) and other artists. This photograph was taken several years after Louis and Fanny met.

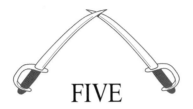

FIVE

The Wild Woman of the West

1876–1879

*A*fter dinner, Lloyd reported, "we all trooped down to the riverside to see the *Cigarette* and the *Arethusa*—the two canoes that had just finished the 'Inland Voyage'—the stranger allowed me to sit in his, and even went to the trouble of setting up the little masts and sails for my amusement. I was very flattered to be treated so seriously."

Lloyd's mother, Fanny Van de Grift Osbourne, was an American art student. She was separated from her husband, who lived in San Francisco.

Louis and Bob, unfamiliar with Americans, were attracted to Fanny's outspoken manner. With dark glowing eyes and a boyish prettiness, she looked much younger than her thirty-five years. Belle resembled her mother so strongly that they were often taken for sisters.

At first Fanny favored Bob, but when Louis, who was twenty-five, fell in love with her, she responded. Even Lloyd sensed the attraction. Louis, whom he called "Luly," told him stories and played with him, pleasing Fanny.

Fanny was born in 1840 in Indianapolis, Indiana. At age sixteen, she married Sam Osbourne. At seventeen she gave birth to Belle. After Sam served on the Union side in the Civil War, the family settled in a silver mining camp in Nevada.

Respectable women were unusual in mining camps, but Fanny was an unusual woman. Like the men around her, she rolled and smoked cigarettes, and learned to shoot well with a heavy revolver. She grew vegetables and sewed pretty dresses for herself and for Belle.

Later the Osbournes moved to California, where they had two sons, Samuel Lloyd, born in 1868, and Hervey, in 1871. Sam was often unfaithful to Fanny, and the couple separated.

In 1875, Fanny gave up on the marriage, taking the children to Europe so that she and Belle, a young lady, could study art. Sam sent small amounts of money to support them.

Fanny and her children went first to Belgium, where the Academy in Antwerp would not admit women. In Paris, however, Fanny found a studio that accepted female students.

Then four-year-old Hervey contracted tuberculosis, and after months of suffering, he died. Grieving, Fanny grew pale and silent. She took Belle and Lloyd to Grez-sur-Loing for the summer, hoping that a change of scene would distract them all.

Belle said, "Louis brought into our lives a sort of joyousness." Dressed like an artist in a peasant blouse and wooden clogs, he would carry Fanny's paints into the woods.

When summer ended, Fanny returned to Paris, to an apartment in Montmartre, the artists' quarter. Louis and Bob visited frequently. To Fanny, both young men seemed surprisingly emotional; either might break into tears or uncontrollable laughter at any time.

Louis still felt ill, and though doctors disagreed on a diagnosis, Fanny decided he had tuberculosis. Louis and Fanny grew closer as she dedicated herself to keeping him healthy.

Louis spent 1877 in Edinburgh, London, and France, writing for a new magazine, *London,* edited by his friend William Henley. Here Louis's short stories "The Rajah's Diamonds" and "The Suicide Club" were published, the latter based on a tale Bob had told at Grez. About this same time, *Cornhill Magazine* began featuring Louis's essays.

Suffering from an eye infection, Louis moved in with Fanny so she could nurse him. When his life seemed threatened, she packed him off to Sidney Colvin's home in London. Fanny charmed Colvin and Mrs. Sitwell, teaching them to roll cigarettes. Louis's other friends were less accepting; Henley, especially, disliked Fanny.

By January 1878, Louis was back in Paris, his thousand pounds spent. He had given up working as a lawyer, but royalties—payments for each copy of his books sold—were low. In addition, Sam had stopped sending Fanny money. Writing to his parents, Louis asked for a larger allowance to support Fanny and her children.

Maggie and Thomas were appalled. Fanny was a married woman! Louis invited Thomas to Paris, where he tried to convince his father that Fanny was honorable, that she had left her marriage only after her husband had behaved outrageously. Thomas, who hoped the affair would end before Fanny could marry his son, raised Louis's allowance. Louis also received a commission, forty-four pounds, for book publication of his *New Arabian Nights* stories from *London* magazine.

In August, Fanny returned to the United States, and Louis, calling himself a "miserable widower," went to the South of France. In September he set off on an eleven-day hike through the Cévennes highlands, a wild, remote area seldom visited by tourists. He hoped that his trip would give him material for another travel book.

During Travels with a Donkey in the Cévennes, *Louis dreamed of Fanny.*

To carry his pack, Louis bought a donkey named Modestine, "a darling, mouse-colour, about the size of a Newfoundland dog . . . costing 65 francs and a glass of brandy." Modestine traveled at her own pace, not Lou's, and his struggles with the animal added comic relief to *Travels with a Donkey in the Cévennes.*

Meanwhile Fanny, Belle, and Lloyd, with Fanny's sister Nellie, went to Oakland, California, where Sam Osbourne worked as a stenographer. Belle and Lloyd, perhaps even Fanny, were glad to see Sam. Sam, still flagrantly unfaithful to his wife, refused to give her a divorce.

Without his love, Louis grew depressed as months passed. He worked on a short story, "The Pavilion on the Links," and wrote a play with Henley, *Deacon Brodie,* about an Edinburgh cabinetmaker who is a master criminal at night. Sometimes Louis doubted that Fanny would ever come back to him.

In July 1879, Fanny sent Louis a telegram. After reading it, Louis bought a ticket for New York.

Louis wrote to Bob on the day he sailed, "Fanny seems to be very ill . . . . I hope to be back in a month or two; but . . . it is a wild world."

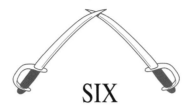

SIX

The Amateur Emigrant

1879–1880

*L*ouis sailed on the SS *Devonia* from Greenock, Scotland, August 7, 1879. He left without saying goodbye to his parents, who expected him to join them at a spa.

As usual Louis wrote a book about his trip, *The Amateur Emigrant,* dedicated to his cousin Bob. In it Louis wrote: "Travel is of two kinds; and this voyage of mine across the ocean combined both. 'Out of my country and myself I go,' sings the old poet: and I was not only travelling out of my country in latitude and longitude, but out of myself in diet, associates, and consideration."

Aboard ship, "in a slantindicular cabin, with the table playing bob-cherry with the ink-bottle," Louis wrote "The Story of a Lie," a short story that sold for fifty pounds.

Though he had paid extra for a cabin, for a place to write, Louis ate with the steerage passengers, the poorest, interviewing them for his book. "The difference between England and America to a working man," Louis said, "was thus most humanely put to me by a fellow-passenger: 'In America,' said he, 'you get pies and puddings.'"

When the ship reached New York on August 18, Louis took a room at a dollar-a-day boarding house. Rain fell steadily the twenty-four hours he was in New York. He wrote to Colvin: "The only American institution which has yet won my respect is the rain. One sees it is a new country, they are so free with their water." Ill and half starved, having lost fourteen pounds on the trip, he itched terribly from a liver ailment.

On the train to California, passengers were "sorted and boxed" into separate cars for families, single men, and Chinese. Louis was shocked by the way Americans treated the Chinese. "Awhile ago it was the Irish," he wrote, "now it is the Chinese that must go. Such is the cry. . . . For my own part, I could not look but with wonder and respect on the Chinese. Their forefathers watched the stars before mine had begun to keep pigs."

Tired and ill, Louis arrived in Monterey, where Fanny lived. Fanny's son Lloyd wrote: "Monterey in 1879 was a sleepy old Mexican town, with most of its buildings of sun-dried bricks, called *adobe*." In this budding artists' colony, Fanny, Belle, Lloyd, and Fanny's sister Nellie lived in an old adobe house surrounded by flowers and fruit trees. Sam Osbourne supported the family and visited from San Francisco on weekends.

Belle recalled coming home one day after an outing to the beach with her beau, artist Joe Strong. "I received the surprise of my life," she said. "Hearing voices in the sitting room I opened the door. And there was Louis Stevenson! I had no idea he was even in the country."

Lloyd described Louis: "His clothes, no longer picturesque but merely shabby, hung loosely on his shrunken body; and there was about him an indescribable lessening of his alertness and self-confidence."

Louis found Fanny recovering from inflammation of the brain, but to his surprise, she refused to resume their relationship. He wrote to Baxter, "My news is nil. I know nothing. I go out camping . . . and now say good-bye to you, having had the itch and a broken heart."

Hunters in the Carmel Valley found him later that week, starving and unconscious, near death. Taking him to their ranch, they cared for him until he could return to Monterey.

Rooming there in a French boarding house, Louis enjoyed the town and its wild coast. His friends were the local doctor, the newspaper editor, and a gentleman bartender, Adolfo Sanchez, who later married Fanny's sister Nellie.

Belle eloped with Joe Strong. She knew Fanny did not approve of an artist for a husband. With Sam Osbourne's help, the young couple moved to San Francisco.

Monterey Square. California was "a land of stagedrivers and highwaymen," said Louis, "like England a hundred years ago."

After months without money, Louis heard from his parents: no more allowance. His new friends took up a collection to pay him two dollars a week as a journalist.

Louis visited Fanny frequently and so did Sam, delighting gossips. Then Fanny moved to Oakland; Louis rented a room in San Francisco, across the bay. Though San Francisco was a rough town, Louis liked it. He wrote well there and walked for miles, meeting sailors and listening to their tales of the South Seas.

Eating in cheap restaurants for seventy cents a day, he suffered from pleurisy and toothaches, but could not afford a dentist. On December 26, 1879, he wrote to Colvin, "For four days I have spoken to no one but to my landlady or landlord or to restaurant waiters. This is not a gay way to pass Christmas, is it? and I must own the guts are a little knocked out of me."

His spirits revived when Fanny decided to come back to him. Sam agreed to a divorce after Fanny promised to see Louis discreetly, in public places, and after she promised to wait a time before remarrying.

To break the news to Lloyd, now eleven, Louis took him for a walk on the beach. Lloyd recalled, "Ordinarily a walk with him was a great treat and a richly imaginative affair, for at a moment's notice I might find myself a pirate, or a redskin, or a young naval officer with secret despatches for a famous spy, or some other similar and tingling masquerade."

This time, however, Louis walked quickly and did not talk. Finally he said, "I want to tell you something. You may not like it, but I hope you will. I am going to marry your mother."

Lloyd said later, "I could not have uttered a word to save my life. I was stricken dumb. The question of whether I were pleased or not did not enter my mind at all. I walked on in a kind of stupefaction, with an uncontrollable impulse to cry—yet I did not cry. . . . all I know is that at last my hand crept into Luly's."

When Louis received a cable that his father was gravely ill, he asked Baxter to check on Thomas, adding, "Since I have gone away I have found out for the first time how I love that man; he is dearer to me than all, except F."

Meanwhile, Thomas asked Colvin to help bring Louis home. "For God's sake," he wrote in a letter, "use your influence. Is it fair that we should be half murdered by his conduct? I am unable to write more about this sinful mad business. . . . I see nothing but destruction to himself as well as to all of us."

In January 1880, the divorce was final. By spring Louis was very ill with signs of tuberculosis: hemorrhaging, or bleeding uncontrollably from the lungs. Coughing up blood, Louis violated the agreement with Sam: he moved in with Fanny and her sister Nellie so they could care for him. Lloyd was at boarding school.

When Thomas, who had recovered, heard his son was dangerously ill, he relented, cabling, "Count on 250 pounds annually." Like Sam, he asked for a delay between the divorce and remarriage.

Louis, feeling better, used some of the money to have his teeth fixed and began dictating a novel, *Prince Otto,* to Nellie. She told how, "while engaged in dictating, he had a habit of walking up and down the room, his pace growing faster and faster as his enthusiasm rose. We feared this was not very good for him, so we quietly devised a scheme to prevent it, without his knowledge, by hemming him in with tables and chairs, so that each time he sprang up to walk he sank back discouraged at sight of the obstructions."

Louis and Fanny were married on May 19, 1880, by a

Presbyterian minister. After exchanging silver wedding bands, the twenty-nine-year-old groom and forty-year-old bride honeymooned in the Napa Valley, a popular spot for tuberculosis patients.

For several months, they lived in Silverado, an old mining town, in a house abandoned by miners. "There were four of us squatters," Louis wrote. He and Fanny were the "King and Queen of Silverado; [Lloyd], the Crown Prince; and Chuchu, the Grand Duke." Chuchu was the dog.

Nellie visited, as did Belle and Joe Strong. "A most good-natured comrade," Lou called Joe, "and a capital hand at an omelette." Louis interviewed his new neighbors, and Lloyd amused himself with a small printing press.

As summer passed, Louis decided to go home to Edinburgh. By this time, his parents wanted to meet Fanny. She had sent them a photo of herself, writing that it was prettier than she was. They welcomed her reports on Louis's health: "As to my dear boy's appearance, he improves every day in the most wonderful way."

Louis, Fanny, and Lloyd sailed from New York on August 7, 1880. In his book *The Silverado Squatters,* Louis wrote of missing Scotland, where, he said, "somehow life is warmer and closer; the hearth burns more redly; the lights of home shine softer on the rainy street; the very names, endeared in verse and music, cling nearer round our hearts."

Louis and Fanny at Silverado, as portrayed by Fanny's son-in-law, Joe Strong. "The place abounded with rattlesnakes," wrote Louis. "The rattlesnakes' nest, it might have been named."

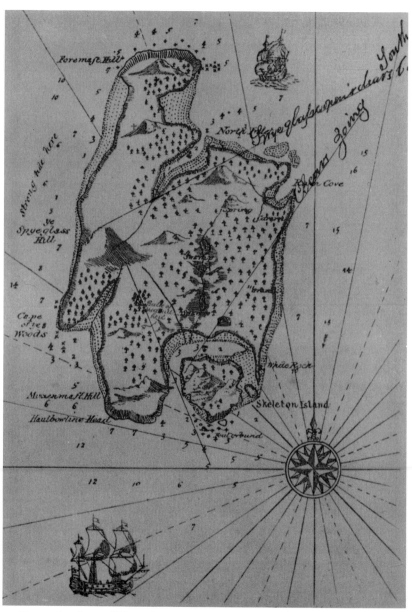

From the first edition of Treasure Island, *a map based on Louis's watercolor painting*

SEVEN

Treasure Island

1880–1882

Sidney Colvin rode the tugboat out to meet the SS *Devonia* as it docked in Liverpool, England, on August 17, 1880. Louis looked thinner to him, except for his cheeks, which were filled out with new teeth.

On the dock, Thomas and Maggie waited. Fanny made a special effort to charm and reassure them. Thomas liked to be teased, she soon learned. She wrote to a friend, "The father is a most lovely old person. He is much better looking I fear than Louis will ever be, and is hustled about, according to the humour of his wife and son, in the most amusing way; occasionally he comes in with twinkling eyes and reports a comic verse of his own making with infinite gusto. Mrs. Stevenson is a much more complex creature, much more like Louis. She is adored by her husband who spoils her like a baby, both I can see, have spoiled Louis."

After years of disapproval, Maggie and Thomas opened their hearts to Fanny and Lloyd. "Fanny fitted into our household from the first," said Maggie.

No. 17 Heriot Row reassured Fanny, who did not share Louis's scorn for material possessions. She enjoyed choosing clothes for him from the many he had left behind.

Seeking a healthful winter climate, Louis, Fanny, and Lloyd set off for Switzerland and the new "alpine" cure recommended for tuberculosis patients. They stopped in London where Fanny received a cool reception from Louis's friends. Colvin wrote to Henley: "[I doubt] whether you and I will ever get used to [Fanny's] little determined brown face and white teeth and grizzling (for that's what it is) grizzling hair."

Fanny called Louis's friends "fiends disguised as friends."

Louis ran out of money in London, but Thomas sent more. Lloyd said that discussions of family finances often ended with the words, "Fanny, I shall have to write to my father."

At Davos, Louis said, "The mountains are about you like a trap."

Finally they arrived at a hotel in Davos, in eastern Switzerland, a mountain village where even the shopkeepers were consumptives—patients with consumption, or tuberculosis. Lloyd said that the saddest part of Davos was the weekly public weigh-in of patients. Luckily Louis gained weight.

He and Fanny stayed aloof from other guests, who regarded Lou's untidy hair and clothes with suspicion, and disapproved of his marriage to a divorcee. Louis wrote:

> FIGURE me to yourself, I pray—
> A man of my peculiar cut—
> Apart from dancing and deray,
> Into an Alpine valley shut;
>
> Shut into a kind of damned Hotel,
> Discountenanced by God and man;
> The food?—Sir, you would do as well
> To cram your belly full of bran.
>
> The company? Alas, the day
> That I should dwell with such a crew,
> With devil anything to say,
> Nor any one to say it to!

In Davos, Louis began a novel set in Scotland in the 1700s. Immersed in histories of the period, he invented a hero, David Balfour, but could not complete the book. He was distracted by an old friend, Mrs. Sitwell. In April 1881, her son Bertie died in Davos at the age of eighteen. Her other son had died of tuberculosis before she met Louis.

Soon after Bertie's death, the Stevensons left Davos for the Scottish Highlands. There Louis became so ill that often he could not speak for fear of hemorrhaging and bleeding to death from his lungs.

Nevertheless he wrote several short stories—"Thrawn

Janet," "The Merry Men," and "The Body Snatcher," the last based on Cummy's stories at the cemetery—for a book of tales of the supernatural. Louis called these stories "crawlers." Fanny was his devoted nurse, first reader, and editor. Though he valued her opinions, he did not always follow her advice.

In August they went to Braemar, Scotland, the town near Queen Victoria's summer residence. They saw the Queen almost every day, riding in an open carriage with her ladies-in-waiting.

When rain kept them indoors, Louis told ghost stories and painted pictures with Lloyd. One day he painted a map of an imaginary place called Treasure Island and invented a story to go with it. He wrote to Henley:

> I am now on another [story] . . . purely owing to Lloyd, this one; but I believe there's more coin in it than in any amount of crawlers . . . 'Treasure Island: A Story for Boys.'
>
> If this don't fetch the kids, why, they have gone rotten since my day. Will you be surprised to learn that it is about Buccaneers, that it begins in the *Admiral Benbow* public-house on Devon coast, that it's all about a map, and a treasure, and a mutiny, and a derelict ship . . . and a sea-cook with one leg, and a sea-song with the chorus 'Yo-ho-ho and a bottle of rum' . . . the trouble is to work it off without oaths. Buccaneers without oaths—brick without straw. But youth and the fond parent have to be consulted.

Louis used the wild coast of Monterey, California, in *Treasure Island,* and based the character of the sea cook with one leg on his friend William Henley. He read the story aloud as he wrote it, reporting to Henley, "All now heard by Lloyd, F., and my father and mother, with high approval. It's quite silly and

Treasure Island *reflects Louis's childhood pirate games. In one of N. C. Wyeth's 1911 illustrations, pirates swarm over a fence.*

horrid fun, and what I want is the best book about the Bucca-
neers that can be had. . . . No women in the story, Lloyd's
orders."

TREASURE ISLAND;

OR,

THE MUTINY OF THE HISPANIOLA.

By CAPTAIN GEORGE NORTH.

PROLOGUE.—THE ADMIRAL BENBOW.

CHAPTER I.

THE OLD SEA DOG AT THE ADMIRAL BENBOW.

QUIRE TRELAWNEY, Dr. Livesey, and the rest of these gentlemen having asked me to write down the whole particulars about Treasure Island, from the beginning to the end, keeping nothing back but the bearings of the island, and that only because there is still treasure not yet lifted, I take up my pen in the year of grace 17—, and go back to the time when my father kept the Admiral Benbow Inn, and the brown old seaman, with the sabre cut, first took up his lodging under our roof. I remember him as if it were yesterday, as he came plodding to the inn door, his sea-chest following behind him in a hand-barrow; a tall, strong, heavy, nut-brown man; his tarry pig-tail falling over the shoulders of his soiled blue coat; his hands ragged and scarred, with black, broken nails; and the sabre cut across one cheek, a dirty, livid white. I remember him looking round the cove and whistling to himself as he did so, and then breaking out in that old sea-song that he sang so often afterwards:

" Fifteen men on the dead man's chest—
Yo-ho-ho, and a bottle of rum. '

Louis used a pen name when Treasure Island *appeared in* Young Folks *magazine, but changed to his real name for book publication.*

Treasure Island was published first in serial installments in *Young Folks* magazine. Louis felt so confident about the story that he allowed the first chapters to be published before the last were written.

That same summer, he read Kate Greenaway's *Birthday Book for Children*. "These are rather nice rhymes," he told Maggie, "and I don't think they would be difficult to do." He began writing poems for children like "The Swing."

How do you like to go up in a swing,
Up in the air so blue?
Oh I do think it is the pleasantest thing
Ever a child can do!

The Stevensons spent their second winter in Davos in a rented chalet. Here Louis wrote well and corresponded with friends, editors, and other authors, taking a keen interest in authors' rights. When one of his publishers suffered a warehouse fire, the company collected damages, but refused to pay authors' royalties on the burned books. Louis wrote to Henley:

Hi O to be a publisher
And be allowed to cheat
For the law that sits on you and me
Lies down and licks his feet.

Louis and Lloyd played war games that lasted for weeks. With colored chalk, they drew maps on the attic floor, creating roads and towns for six hundred miniature lead soldiers.

Lloyd described his stepfather: "A more delightful playfellow never lived; my memory of that winter is one of extraordinary entertainment. He engraved blocks and wrote poems for the two tiny books I printed on my press; he painted scenery for my toy theatre . . . helped me to give performances and slide the actors in and out on their tin stands, as well as imitating galloping horses, or screaming screams for the heroine in distress. My mother, usually the sole audience, would laugh till she had to be patted on the back."

Mr. Hyde changes back into Dr. Jekyll, as illustrated by William Hole in 1899. "I've got my shilling shocker," Louis reported happily.

EIGHT

Dr. Jekyll & Mr. Hyde

1883–1887

Louis and Fanny spent the next winter in France. In March 1883, they rented a cottage, the Châlet La Solitude, in Hyères, overlooking the Mediterranean Sea. Louis told Mrs. Sitwell that it was the "loveliest house you ever saw, with a garden like a fairy story, and a view like a classical landscape." The weather, he said, was "cloudless, clear as crystal, with just a punkah-draft of the most aromatic air, all pine and gum tree."

Dressing like a Frenchman in a short black cape, Louis sported a small beard, called an Imperial. His hair had darkened over the years to blackish brown.

In Hyères, Louis worked on two novels at the same time. The hero in *Prince Otto,* who loses his throne and retreats to the forest to write poetry, combined the personalities of Louis and his cousin Bob. Louis patterned other characters in the book after Fanny, Thomas, and the elder Russian sister he had met at Menton. He made the fictional Countess von Rosen less bawdy than her real-life counterpart.

Louis loved *Prince Otto,* which he had started writing in California. He was less interested in *The Black Arrow,* a tale of the Wars of the Roses in fifteenth-century England, written as a serial for *Young Folks* magazine. Their proofreader helped by notifying Louis that he had lost track of several characters and that he had forgotten what happened to the fourth black arrow.

During this same time, Louis wrote more children's poems for *A Child's Garden of Verses.*

Rain

The rain is raining all around,
It falls on field and tree,
It rains on the umbrellas here,
And on the ships at sea.

My Shadow

I have a little shadow that goes in and out with me,
And what can be the use of him is more than I can see.
He is very, very like me from the heels up to the head;
And I see him jump before me, when I jump into my bed.

The funniest thing about him is the way he likes to grow—
Not at all like proper children, which is always very slow;
For he sometimes shoots up taller like an india-rubber ball,
And he sometimes gets so little that there's none of him at all.

He hasn't got a notion of how children ought to play,
And can only make a fool of me in every sort of way.
He stays so close beside me, he's a coward you can see;
I'd think shame to stick to nursie as that shadow sticks to me!

One morning, very early, before the sun was up,
I rose and found the shining dew on every buttercup;
But my lazy little shadow, like an arrant sleepy-head,
Had stayed at home behind me and was fast asleep in bed.

On May 5, 1883, Louis wrote to his parents: "MY DEAR-EST PEOPLE,—I have had a great piece of news. There has been offered for *Treasure Island*—how much do you suppose? I believe it would be an excellent jest to keep the answer till my next letter. For two cents I would do so. Shall I? Anyway, I'll turn the page first. No—well—A hundred pounds, all alive, O! A hundred jingling, tingling, golden, minted quid. Is not this wonderful?"

The book *Treasure Island,* dedicated to "Lloyd Osbourne, an American Gentleman," established Louis as a best-selling author.

Jessie Wilcox Smith illustrated A Child's Garden of Verses *in 1905. This drawing depicts "My Shadow."*

In 1884, Lloyd joined Louis and Fanny in Hyères after a year away at school. At age sixteen, he was tall, blond, near-sighted, and fascinated by gadgets like cameras and type-writers. He began typing Louis's manuscripts.

Fanny gardened at Hyères, growing exotic, American vegetables that Louis liked to eat. She was a grandmother now; Belle and Joe Strong had a baby son, Austin. Fanny was often ill in Hyères; sometimes it seemed that she got sick whenever Louis did. Valentine Roche, their cook and maid, cared for both and entertained the family with her lively sense of humor. For six years, she shared their table, their travels, and their friends. Louis suffered from hemorrhages, malaria, sciatica, and an eye infection, but even when his eyes were bandaged, he refused to be treated like an invalid. "Oh, hell," he said, "what does it matter? Let me die with my boots on." When he could not talk, he communicated with hand signals or by writing notes. "Don't be frightened," he wrote to Fanny. "If this is death, it is an easy one."

Fanny limited his visitors to a few minutes and isolated him from people with colds. She was right to do so, but this practice seemed unusual and irritated his parents and friends.

Louis wrote to his mother about Fanny: "She is every-thing to me; wife, brother, sister, daughter and dear compan-ion; and I would not change to get a goddess or a saint."

When cholera broke out in Hyères, Louis, Fanny, and Valentine moved to Bournemouth, England, a health spa on the south coast where Lloyd went to school. In 1885, Thomas gave Fanny and Louis a wedding present of a house and five hundred pounds for furnishings. Fanny chose a yellow brick villa with a blue slate roof, on a cliff overlooking the sea. Louis named it Skerryvore after a famous Stevenson lighthouse, and placed a model lighthouse at the street entrance.

SKERRYVORE

H ere all is sunny and when the truant gull
Skims the green level of the lawn, his wing
Dispetals roses; here the house is framed
Of kneaded brick and the plumed mountain pine,
Such clay as artists fashion and such wood
As the tree-climbing urchin breaks.

Skerryvore, Fanny's "lovely luxurious little nest," was destroyed
by a German bomb in the second World War.

When the famous American author Henry James brought his ailing sister to Bournemouth, he called on Louis at Skerryvore. The two had corresponded over literary matters. James returned to Skerryvore so often that Louis and Fanny held a formal christening for "Henry James's chair."

Visitors exhausted Louis, especially his friend William Henley. Lloyd described Henley as "a great, glowing, massive-shouldered fellow with a big red beard and a crutch; jovial, astoundingly clever, and with a laugh that rolled out like music. . . . He had an unimaginable fire and vitality; he swept one off one's feet."

To Fanny, Henley was a "rowdy, roaring, hairy, bulky Old Man of the Sea on Louis' frail back." But she agreed that Louis and Henley should write plays together because she thought plays earned more money than books. After three plays failed, Fanny blamed Henley and he blamed her.

Giving up plays, Louis studied Scottish history. A book called *The Trial of James Stewart* inspired him to try to finish his Scottish novel of the 1700s, begun in Davos. He wrote to his father, "I am at David [the hero] again . . . have just murdered James Stewart semi-historically."

In *Kidnapped,* set in 1751, David Balfour, a poor Scottish orphan, is kidnapped by his wicked uncle and imprisoned on a ship bound for America. David escapes to the Scottish Highlands with Alan Breck Stewart, a wanted man. Though their political views differ, they help each other. *Kidnapped,* dedicated to Charles Baxter, achieved great acclaim.

Despite his success, Louis still needed help from Thomas to support his family. He was outraged to learn that publishers had reissued his books in the United States without paying him royalties for each copy of his books they sold.

A Child's Garden of Verses, first published in 1885, was

David Balfour, washed overboard in a shipwreck. Kidnapped *illustration is by N. C. Wyeth.*

dedicated "To Alison Cunningham From Her Boy." Visiting Cummy, Louis said to her, before a room full of people: "It's you that gave me the passion for the drama."

"Me, Master Lou?" protested Cummy. "I never put foot inside a play-house in all my life!"

"Ay, woman," he replied, "but it was the grand dramatic way ye had of reciting the hymns!"

At Bournemouth, Louis began a new book. Lloyd reported: "One day [Louis] came down to luncheon in a very preoccupied frame of mind, hurried through his meal—an unheard-of thing for him to do—and on leaving said he was working with extraordinary success on a new story that had come to him in a dream, and that he was not to be interrupted or disturbed even if the house caught fire."

Sitting in bed, Louis wrote furiously. For three days, the household tiptoed and whispered, until he was ready to read the story aloud.

It told of a seemingly respectable Dr. Jekyll, who invented a potion that transformed him into another person, Mr. Hyde. Mr. Hyde was a bestial murderer. Lloyd said, "I listened to it spellbound. Stevenson, who had a voice the greatest actor might have envied, read it with an intensity that made shivers run up and down my spine. When he came to the end, gazing at us in triumphant expectancy and keyed to a pitch of indescribable self-satisfaction—as he waited, and I waited, for my mother's outburst of enthusiasm—I was thunderstruck at her backwardness. Her praise was constrained; the words seemed to come with difficulty; and then all at once she broke out with criticism."

Fanny urged Louis to recast the story, making the wicked Dr. Jekyll a good man who has trouble controlling his evil instincts. Then, she explained, Dr. Jekyll would represent the dual nature of Victorian society: prim and proper on the surface, unrestrained and lewd underneath.

Louis, his voice "bitter and challenging," shouted Fanny

down in a "fury of resentment." Lloyd had never seen him "so impassioned, so outraged." Later Lloyd found Fanny alone, pale and desolate.

Then Louis returned, saying, "You are right! I have absolutely missed . . . the whole point of it—the very essence of it." To their dismay, he threw his manuscript into the fire!

He rewrote the story, sixty-four thousand words, in six days, following Fanny's advice. *The Strange Case of Dr. Jekyll and Mr. Hyde,* dedicated to Louis's cousin Katherine De Mattos (Bob's sister), brought Louis great fame, even with people who had not read it. His characters became known throughout the English-speaking world.

Thomas Stevenson died in 1887, leaving his son three thousand pounds sterling. There would be no more allowance.

In July 1887, after Louis suffered "horrifying" hemorrhages, doctors suggested the new American mountain cure, in New Mexico or Colorado. Widow Maggie, now fifty-eight, accepted an invitation to accompany Louis, Fanny, Lloyd, and Valentine to the United States.

At Bournemouth, Louis called himself "a miserable snuffling, shivering, fever-stricken, nightmare-ridden, knee jottering, hoast-hoast-hoasting shadow and remains of man."

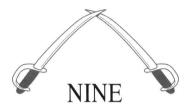

NINE

Where the Golden Apples Grow

1887–1888

*T*o save money, Fanny bought tickets on a freighter instead of a passenger ship. The SS *Ludgate* sailed from London, stopping in Le Havre, France, to take on surprising freight: apes bound for American zoos, cattle, and 240 horses. Louis said, "The stallions stood hypnotised by the motion [of the ship], looking through the ports at our dinner-table and winked when the crockery was broken . . . and the big monkey, Jacko, scoured about the ship and rested willingly in my arms, to the ruin of my clothing."

Eleven days later, as the ship approached New York Harbor, a pilot boat came out to meet it. Maggie wrote, "the pilot was greatly delighted when he found out who Louis was; it seems that he himself actually went by the name of 'Mr. Hyde' on board the pilot-boat, and his partner was called Dr. Jekyll, because the one was easy and good-natured, and the other rather hard."

Louis's story was as popular in the United States as in Britain. A "Jekyll and Hyde" play opened in New York to great acclaim soon after Louis arrived. Though American copyright laws did not protect Louis, a British citizen, the play's producer paid him voluntarily for the use of his book.

In a New York hotel, the famous author held a press conference, urging readers to buy only authorized editions of his works. Publishers called with tempting offers; Louis accepted one from *Scribner's* magazine: seven hundred pounds for a series of essays.

After pricing travel to the West and worrying that high altitudes might damage Fanny's health, the family went instead to the Adirondack Mountains in New York. They rented a house in Saranac, a resort town popular with "lungers," as

At Saranac, left to right, *were Valentine Roche, a local maid, Lloyd, Fanny, and Louis, who called himself "a rank Saranacker and a wild man of the woods."*

tuberculosis patients were known there. Though Louis benefited from treatments prescribed for consumptives, doctors disagreed on whether he really had tuberculosis.

Before winter set in, Fanny went to Montreal, the nearest city, to shop for buffalo coats, sealskin boots, and fur caps.

At Saranac, Louis received an upsetting letter from William Henley. Fanny, Henley complained, had taken a story by Louis's cousin Katherine De Mattos, rewritten it slightly, then published it as her own work in *Scribner's* magazine. "Why there wasn't a double signature," wrote Henley, "is what I've not been able to understand."

Louis, who believed that Fanny had acted honorably, with Katherine's permission, wrote to Charles Baxter, "God knows if I heard ill of Henley's wife, I should bottle it up in my heart from him. . . . If this be friendship, I am not robust enough to bear it."

Despite his sadness over quarreling with his close friend, Louis thrived at Saranac. The thermometer sometimes dropped to forty below zero, but on warmer days, Louis went sleigh riding and ice skating.

Editor Charles McClure skated with Louis when he visited Saranac. Together they hatched a fantastic scheme: McClure would charter a yacht for Louis, paying expenses for a South Pacific cruise, and Louis would send back travel reports to be published in the United States and Britain. Lloyd, they decided, would take photos on the trip and record sounds with a recording phonograph.

In *A Child's Garden of Verses,* Louis had written:

> I should like to rise and go
> Where the golden apples grow;—
> Where below another sky
> Parrot islands anchored lie.

Now he pored over maps and *Findlay's Directories of the World.* These books guided sailors into remote bays by describing landmarks like "a peculiarly shaped rock, not unlike a stranded whale," and told where to find freshwater and pigs.

Fanny went to San Francisco to see her daughter Belle and sister Nellie, and to look for a yacht. In Saranac the clatter of Lloyd's typewriter keys filled the cottage. At age eighteen, he had decided to become a writer.

Louis praised one of Lloyd's stories: "it is really not at all bad," he said. "Some of it is devilishly funny." Then Louis offered to "make it *sing,*" and the result was a short story by both of them, "The Wrong Box." Publishing jointly with Lloyd, a United States citizen, provided Louis with copyright protection in both America and Britain.

In December, Louis began a new novel, *The Master of Ballantrae.* Like *Jekyll & Hyde,* it was a study in duality. Louis said that the story "leads up to the death of the elder brother at the hands of the younger in a perfectly cold-blooded murder, of which I wish (and mean) the reader to approve."

In May, Fanny sent Louis a telegram: "Can secure splendid sea-going schooner yacht *Casco* for seven hundred and fifty a month with most comfortable accommodation for six aft and six forward. Can be ready for sea in ten days. Reply immediately."

"Blessed girl," Louis wired in return, "take the yacht and expect us in ten days."

Secundra digs up his master's grave in The Master of Ballantrae, *illustrated by William Hole. "This cursed end of* The Master *hangs over me like the arm of the gallows, but it is always darkest before dawn," wrote Louis, who had trouble finishing the book.*

Crossing the Pacific on the Casco, Louis said, "Day after day, the sun flamed, night after night, the moon beaconed, or the stars paraded their lustrous regiment."

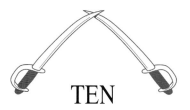

TEN

To the Cannibal Islands: The Voyage of the *Casco*

1888–1889

*T*he *Casco* was a ninety-five-foot schooner with elaborate carvings, gilded mirrors, crimson sofas, and a red carpet. More suited for racing than crossing the ocean, it had once sailed to Tahiti. The *Casco*'s owner, Samuel Merritt, worried about leasing his ship to a bohemian writer. He insisted they use his captain.

Captain A. H. Otis did not want the charter. Having read *Treasure Island,* he disapproved of its sailing scenes. He hated "fashionable yacht-sailing" and deplored women on ships. Asked what he would do if the elderly Maggie fell overboard, the gruff captain replied, "Put it in the log."

But Louis charmed Merritt, who told Otis, "Why, Captain, Mr. Stevenson seems quite as sensible a man as you or I," and finally Otis agreed to take them.

In San Francisco, the Stevensons saw Fanny's daughter Belle and her seven-year-old son Austin. Belle and Joe Strong had moved their family to Honolulu, where Joe had achieved modest success as an artist. But the marriage was troubled; Joe drank heavily and spent money so recklessly that Belle had to appeal to Louis for financial support.

Belle offered practical advice for their voyage: Fanny, Maggie, and their maid Valentine needed *holaku,* she said, "Mother Hubbard" dresses that hung from the shoulders, long and full. Underneath, women wore *muumuus,* or petticoats, but no corsets. Missionaries had introduced the style to women who formerly had worn very little.

On June 26, 1888, a tug pulled the *Casco* away from a boatload of reporters, past the Golden Gate Bridge. They were off for the French Marquesas, the easternmost islands in Polynesia.

Fanny, Lloyd, and Valentine spent the first three days sick in their bunks, but Louis, on his first morning at sea, ate a large breakfast of red herrings and mutton chops. Maggie, also a good sailor, described the *Casco:* "From the deck you step down into the cockpit which is our open-air drawing-room. It has seats all round, nicely cushioned, and we sit or lie there most of the day. The compass is there, and the wheel, so the man at the wheel always keeps us company. . . . After dinner we go on deck for the sunset, which is the great spectacle of the day."

Captain Otis told Fanny, "*Please* don't talk to the man at the wheel today, Mrs. Stevenson. *Today* I want him to steer." But she could not resist instructing the ship's crew, especially the drunken cook, and even Otis liked the food better after she intervened. Fanny and Maggie won Otis's respect with their toughness and their skill at whist, a card game that occupied many hours at sea.

As the weather grew warmer, Maggie wrote, "Louis goes

about in shirt and trousers, and with bare feet: he and Lloyd got their faces and arms so tanned at the beginning that they must now be surely sunproof."

At night, new stars came into view: the Southern Cross. Soon the *Casco* reached the French Marquesas, a group of twelve "high" or volcanic islands, with mountains rising thousands of feet above the sea.

On July 28, they dropped anchor off the island of Nuka-hiva. Canoes from the village of Anaho met the ship, bringing the island chief, a German trader, and many other men, nearly naked. Maggie said, "The display of legs was something we were not accustomed to; but as they were all tattooed in most wonderful patterns, it really looked quite as if they were wearing open-work silk tights."

Louis worried when he saw the ship full of men, "all talking, and we could not understand one word; all trying to trade with us who had no thought of trading, or offering us island curios at prices palpably absurd."

When the Stevensons refused to buy, Louis said, "complaint ran high and rude; and one [man], the jester of the party, railed upon our meanness amid jeering laughter. . . . The ship was manifestly in their power; we had women on board; I knew nothing of my guests beyond the fact that they were cannibals."

Later Louis laughed at his fears. He made friends with the Marquesans, speaking French to some, studying their language, too, and communicating without words. "I was the showman of the *Casco*," he said. The ship's "fine lines, tall spars, and snowy decks, the crimson fittings of the saloon, and the white, the gilt, and the repeating mirrors of the tiny cabin, brought us a hundred visitors."

For six weeks, Louis explored Nuka-hiva. Marquesan houses stood on huge stone platforms, four to eight feet above the ground, reached by broad stairs. Some had running water, brought down the mountains in bamboo pipes. "In the hour of the dusk," Louis reported, "when the fire blazes and the scent of the cooked breadfruit fills the air . . . you shall behold them silently assemble to this meal, men, women, and children; and the dogs and pigs frisk together up the terrace stairway, switching rival tails. The strangers from the ship were soon equally welcome: welcome to dip their fingers in the wooden dish, to drink cocoa-nuts, to share the circulating pipe, and to hear and hold high debate about the misdeeds of the French, the Panama Canal, or the geographical position of San Francisco and New Yo'ko. In a Highland hamlet, quite out of reach of any tourist, I have met the same plain and dignified hospitality."

Controlled by the French, the Marquesas were heavily influenced by Catholic missionaries. Though human sacrifice had been banned for several years, Louis visited the former killing site known as the high place. In the past, he learned, islanders had eaten their enemies. When no enemies were available, they had sacrificed least-liked members of their own clans. They had killed unwanted babies, too.

When Queen Vaekebu visited the *Casco,* her tattooed hands reminded Louis of lace mittens worn by elderly ladies in Britain. As he told her goodbye, Louis thought, "This was a queen of cannibals. . . . she had sat on the high place . . . while the drums were going twenty strong and the priests carried up the bloodstained baskets of long-pig." The Queen had become a Catholic, and quite religious, Louis learned.

Another guest, Chief Kooamua, was known as the last eater of "long-pig" in Nuka-hiva. "Not many years have elapsed," wrote Louis, "since he was seen striding on the

Islanders visit the Casco. *Though Louis complained of "villainous tinned foods" on board ship, his guests enjoyed tasting them.*

beach of Anaho, a dead man's arm across his shoulder. 'So does Kooamua to his enemies!' he roared to the passers-by, and took a bite from the raw flesh."

Maggie said of the chief: "the thing that charmed him most was the typewriter. He went off at last, very happy, with a *Casco* ribbon for his hat, a piece of plug tobacco in his pocket, and his name and that of every member of his family printed by himself with the typewriter."

Louis used Scottish history and Cummy's Covenanter stories to help him understand the Marquesans. He said, "points of similarity between a South Sea people and some of

my own folk at home ran much in my head in the islands . . . . When I desired any detail of savage custom, or of
superstitious belief, I cast back in the story of my fathers, and
fished for what I wanted with some trait of equal barbarism."

Like the ancient Scots, Marquesans organized their society by family clans around powerful chiefs. A chief could
tapu—make taboo, or forbid—anything that went against
common interest. Thus a chief might tapu a popular fishing
reef to keep it from getting fished out. The French had outlawed tapus and tattoos, believing these customs were related
to cannibalism, but Louis observed that "the tapu is . . . often
the instrument of wise and needful restrictions."

In 1889, Nuka-hiva's population was shrinking. Many
dwelling platforms stood empty and overgrown, their inhabi-
tants dead from smallpox, tuberculosis, and other western
diseases, and from human sacrifice and infanticide. In forty
years, the population in one district had declined from six
thousand to less than four hundred.

Frightened and discouraged, obsessed with death, many
of the remaining islanders were so sad that they had given up
trying to work. Some sought comfort in opium, and suicide
was common.

"When the people sang for us in Anaho," reported Louis,
"they must apologise for the smallness of their repertory.
They were only young folk present, they said, and it was only
the old that knew the songs. The whole body of Marquesan
poetry and music was being suffered to die out with a single
dispirited generation."

From the Marquesas, the *Casco* sailed to the Paumotus,
known also as the "Dangerous Islands" because navigation
there was so difficult. Captain Otis had fired their drunken
cook and hired a young Chinese man named Ah Fu in his place.

In October the *Casco* sailed to the Society Islands, or Tahiti, where the travelers spent several weeks in the village of Tautira, in a "bird-cage" house, with walls of split bamboo.

Louis made friends with the local chief, Ori a Ori. Six foot three, with a huge mustache, Ori, who spoke French and En-

Tautira, Tahiti. "We are in heaven here," Louis wrote, after the people sang to him on a warm November night.

glish, taught Louis the Tahitian language. Following local custom, Louis "made brothers" with Ori by exchanging names with him, stating that the chief "is now called Rui, the nearest they can come to Louis, for they have no *l* and no *s* in their language."

In Tahiti, Fanny and Maggie learned to plait hats; Lloyd took photographs; Valentine practiced cooking outside. Maggie attended Protestant church services and learned to type, then she and Lloyd typed Louis's diary each morning.

Louis worked on *The Master of Ballantrae* and wrote to Sidney Colvin, "I got wonderful materials for my [South Seas] book, collected songs and legends on the spot; songs still sung in chorus by perhaps a hundred persons, not two of whom can agree on their translation; legends, on which I have seen half a dozen seniors sitting in conclave and debating what came next."

With the help of a translator, he told the Tahitians Covenanter tales from Scotland and entertained them by playing the flageolet, a small woodwind instrument.

The *Casco*'s last stop on the tour was to be Honolulu, in the Sandwich Islands, or Hawaii. Louis wrote to Colvin:

> O, how my spirit languishes
> To step ashore on the Sanguishes;
> For there my letters wait,
> There shall I know my fate.

In November he wrote to his friend Charles Baxter, "Whether I have a penny left in the wide world, I know not, nor shall know, till I get to Honolulu." The mail he expected included his royalty checks.

But their departure was delayed when the *Casco* needed repairs. Otis took the ship to the Tahitian capital city of

Papeete to have the work done. He was due back in two
weeks; after a month, Louis's family feared Otis had deserted
them. They worried about Belle, too, waiting for them in Honolulu, wondering where they were.

When their supplies ran out, the Stevensons turned to
Ori a Ori for help. Both Louis and Fanny wept in this emotional conversation.

"I know that your food is done," Ori replied, "but I can
give you fish and *fei* [red bananas] as much as you like. This
place suits you, and it makes us happy to have you,—stay
here till the *Casco* comes, be happy, *et ne pleurez plus* [don't
cry any more]!"

Finally Otis returned with the ship repaired and restocked, and they sailed on Christmas Day.

Four weeks later, Honolulu officials declared the *Casco*
lost at sea.

"We are here in the suburb of Honolulu in a rambling house,"
Louis wrote. "The town is some three miles away, but the house is
connected by telephone with the chief shops, and the tramway
runs to within a quarter of a mile of us."

ELEVEN

The Sandwich Islands

1889

*T*he voyage to Honolulu was so rough that sometimes the *Casco's* sailors had to be tied to the deck to keep them from falling overboard. In the cabin, passengers held on constantly to avoid being thrown about.

Their excitement at sighting the island of Oahu turned to disappointment as the ship was becalmed for three days. Sitting motionless outside the harbor, the travelers ate their last salt beef and biscuit, watching the lights of Honolulu at night.

Finally Belle, who had heard they were coming, reported: "The *Casco,* all sails set, came flying round Diamond Head with the speed of an express train. Austin [her son] and I were in a little open boat directly in her path. Why we were not run down and drowned is a mystery to me.

"I can't remember how we got on board, but in the midst of shouts and screams we were scooped out of our boat and found ourselves sprawling on the deck, Louis and Lloyd laughing as they helped us to our feet."

Maggie wrote: "I must confess our dinner that night at

the hotel seemed to me the very finest banquet of which I had ever partaken. But, oh dear me, this place is so civilised! And to come back from Tautira to telephones and electric light is at first very bewildering and unpleasant."

In the mail, Louis found checks! He rented a house at Waikiki, a small beach settlement of about twenty-five families. The *lanai,* or open-sided sitting-room, had trellises for walls, covered with flowers and vines. There Joe Strong painted, Lloyd typed "The Wrong Box," and Maggie pasted clippings about Louis into scrapbooks. Fanny decorated the house with mats and shells and rented a grand piano. Ah Fu, now Fanny's devoted friend, cooked in a separate building, planted a garden, and played with eight-year-old Austin.

Leaving the Stevensons, Captain Otis took the *Casco* back to San Francisco. Their maid Valentine, tired of life with the demanding Fanny, returned to California, and Maggie sailed for Scotland to see her ailing sister Jane.

At Waikiki, Louis wrote in a small, cobwebby shack lined with mildewed newspapers. Lloyd said: "Here in complete contentment, with his cot, flageolet, and ink-bottle, he set himself to the task of finishing the 'Master of Ballantrae'— while centipedes wriggled unnoticed on his floor, lizards darted after flies, and the undisturbed spiders peacefully continued the weaving of their webs. Here King Kalakaua [the King of the Sandwich Islands] would occasionally drop in on him for a long and confidential talk, while the horses of the royal equipage flicked their tails under a neighboring tree and the imposing coachman and footman dozed on their box."

Louis liked the handsome young king, a world traveler who was modernizing his country while preserving traditional culture. The king's enemies were the missionaries, who spread false rumors about him: that he was a drunkard and a

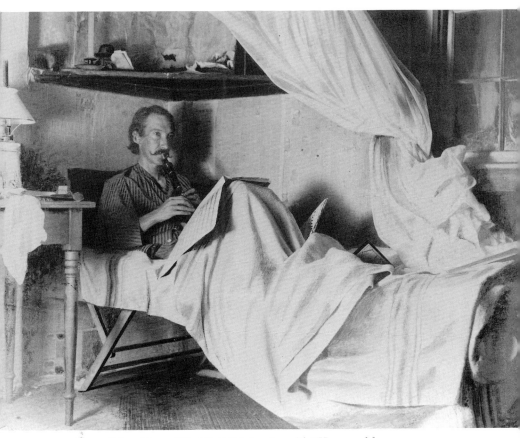

Describing himself in Waikiki, Louis said, "He now blows a flageolet with singular effects: sometimes the poor thing appears stifled with shame, sometimes it screams with agony."

spendthrift, and that he gave wild parties called orgies. Belle explained, "the word 'missionary' had a political significance like Democrat or Republican. The leaders were the sons and grandsons of the original missionaries who came to Hawaii to convert the heathen. They were rich, prosperous American business men with one aim: to wrest the islands from the natives and have it taken over by the United States."

Lloyd, Fanny, Louis and Maggie entertain King Kalakaua in the cabin of the Casco. *The King had read Louis's books.*

King Kalakaua and his followers, including Belle and Joe Strong, were known as the royal set. Louis joined the group, but he befriended missionaries, too. Because everyone, it seemed, wanted to meet him, he established regular "afternoons" at home. Socializing amused him after so many years when illness had kept him shut in "like a weevil in a biscuit."

At Waikiki, Louis planned a second voyage. They would sail to the Gilberts, a string of sixteen "low" islands, or coral reefs, on a commercial ship, the *Equator.* This sixty-four-foot schooner traded a variety of goods for copra. Copra, or dried coconut meat, yielded coconut oil, and was the main cash crop of the Pacific. Captain Denis Reid, a charming young Scotsman, asked Ah Fu to be ship's cook for the four-month tour.

Their supplies included revolvers, cigars, vegetable seeds, a portable organ, hammocks, a magic lantern [slide projector], religious and comic slides, Louis's flageolet, Fanny's guitar, and Lloyd's "taro-patch fiddle," probably a ukulele. Preparing for the trip, Belle and Fanny made wreaths of artificial flowers to give to islanders. These were popular on low islands, where few plants grew.

Meanwhile, Joe Strong's drinking, combined with drug abuse, had grown so outrageous that he was said to have suffered a nervous breakdown. Louis and Fanny decided to take him with them, to try to straighten him out, and he agreed to paint transparencies of scenery for magic lantern slides. Belle was to take Austin to Sydney, Australia, where Louis would send her money.

On June 24, 1889, as the *Equator* prepared to cast off, two fine carriages "drove down at full speed to the wharf and there deposited King Kalakaua and a party of native musicians. . . . The king . . . stood there waving his hand, while from the musicians, lined up on the very edge of the wharf, came the tender strains of a farewell."

Belle and Austin also waved from the dock. Belle wrote of her husband, Joe: "After his illness he was never the same again. . . . He and I began to get on each other's nerves more and more, till it was a positive relief to see him sail away."

The King's band played "Aloha Oe" to Lloyd, Louis, and Fanny as
the Equator *sailed from Honolulu.*

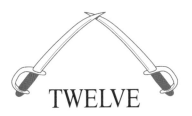

TWELVE

To the Gilbert Islands: The Voyage of the *Equator*

1889

*A*s he traveled, Louis mailed reports to Sam McClure, and McClure had them published in the New York *Sun*. Someday, Louis planned, these reports would be chapters in a "prose-epic" on the South Seas. His subject was tragic, he said: the "unjust (yet I can see the inevitable) extinction of the Polynesian Islanders by our shabby civilization."

Fanny complained to Colvin, "Louis has the most enchanting material that any one ever had in the whole world for his book, and I am afraid he is going to spoil it all. He has taken into his Scotch-Stevenson head that a stern duty lies before him, and that his book must be a sort of scientific and historical, impersonal thing." Readers wanted light-hearted travelogues, Fanny insisted, not scholarly essays on language, politics, and Western oppression. By letter Colvin agreed, but Louis refused to change.

After thirty-four installments, the New York *Sun* pulled

out of the contract with McClure, saying the reports were "not what they asked for . . . but only the advance sheets of a book and rather a dull book at that." Louis received only a partial payment. Though he never abandoned the South Seas book, he had to sell other titles to support his family.

On board the *Equator,* Louis and Lloyd began a new novel together, *The Wrecker.* Based on a true story Louis had heard in Hawaii, it told of sailors shipwrecked, then rescued and brought to Honolulu. Set in Scotland, Fontainebleau, San Francisco, the Marquesas, and Hawaii, the book followed Louis's travels. One character, Captain Nares, resembled the *Casco*'s Captain Otis. *The Wrecker* sold for fifteen thousand dollars.

The *Equator*'s first stop, on July 14, 1889, was on Butaritari, in the Gilberts. Louis, Fanny, Lloyd, and Joe Strong

Butaritari Island, in the Gilberts. "What is the meaning of all this?" Louis asked on arrival. "Is the island on a spree?"

waded ashore. To their surprise, they found most of the islanders either asleep or drunk.

The island was controlled by the United States, so King Tebureioma had raised the *tapu* against drinking to celebrate Independence Day, July 4. Ten days later, three white traders were still selling liquor and the party had turned to a "debauch." Tebureioma, also drunk, maintained order by firing a rifle over the head of anyone who displeased him, and the King's bodyguards did the same.

Shocked at the sight of "king, magistrates, police, and army joining in one common scene of drunkenness," Louis wrote, "It was a serious question that night if we should sleep ashore. But we were travellers, folk that had come far in quest of the adventurous; on the first sign of adventure it would have been a singular inconsistency to have withdrawn; and we sent on board instead for our revolvers." These they used for target practice on the public highway, firing at bottles, impressing people with their marksmanship. Fanny, an excellent shot, was much admired.

They stayed at a missionary's house, which the king *tapued* to protect them, under a fine of fifty dollars. On two nights, when they lit a lamp at dusk, rocks came flying through the window.

Louis urged the traders to stop selling alcohol, but they feared more violence if they did. Finally the king re-enforced the *tapu* peacefully. Order restored, the islanders entertained their visitors with a concert, and Louis and Lloyd gave a slide show. The audience was amazed to see "phantoms" of Bible history, which they took to be photographs—proof that the Bible was true.

From Butaritari the *Equator* sailed to Apemama so Louis could meet King Tembinok', ruler of three islands. The

"Napoleon of the Gilberts," as Tembinok' was known, had saved his islands from Western interference by outshooting a British warship. All copra on his islands belonged to him.

Tolerating whites on his own terms, Tembinok' had allowed a missionary to stay long enough to teach him English. He welcomed a few white traders and visitors, like Louis, who could teach him about the outside world.

"We were scarce yet moored," wrote Louis, "before distant and busy figures appeared upon the beach, a boat was launched, and a crew pulled out to us bringing the king's ladder." Lashed to the *Equator*, the ladder looked large and sturdy.

Then a man-of-war left the beach and delivered Tembinok' to their ship. Tall and fat, the king was about forty-five years old, with a beaked profile and a mane of long black hair. Tembinok' was known for his unusual attire: flowered neckties, red drawers, green velvet coats, and elaborate evening gowns. Louis reported: "Where there are no fashions, none to set them, few to follow them if they were set, and none to criticise, [Tembinok'] dresses . . . 'to his own heart.'" Even Louis thought that in a dress, the king looked "ominous and weird beyond belief."

Tembinok's subjects were nearly naked. Women in the Gilberts still wore the "ridi," described by Louis as "a cutty petticoat or fringe of the smoked fibre of cocoa-nut leaf . . . the lower edge not reaching the mid-thigh, the upper adjusted so low upon the haunches that it seems to cling by accident. A sneeze, you think, and the lady must surely be left destitute."

Tembinok' gave them permission to stay three weeks, while the ship went on without them. The king ordered four houses for their use, moved to a site near a pond. Lloyd described an Apemama house: "a sort of giant clothes-basket...with a peaked roof, and standing on stilts about a

King Tembinok', said Louis, "would come strolling over, always alone, a little before meal-time, take a chair, and talk and eat with us like an old family friend."

yard high. With a dozen pairs of human legs under it, you can steer it to any spot you like—provided it is level—and begin your modest housekeeping without further fuss."

Fanny lined the main house with mosquito netting and planted vegetable seeds outside. Tembinok' loaned them furniture, and visited often, usually at dinnertime.

Louis called on Tembinok', too, pleasing the king's wives by playing a card game Tembinok' had invented. The king quizzed Louis on Western ways: etiquette, government, law, police, money, medicine. In Apemama, he enforced the law by firing over the heads of offenders, or at their feet. "I am told the king is a crack shot;" wrote Louis, "that when he aims to kill, the grave may be got ready."

Tembinok' did sometimes kill people, including one of his wives. He had left her remains putrefying in an open box before the palace gate, to serve as a warning to others.

Three weeks passed pleasantly, and the ship did not come; after six weeks there was still no sign of the *Equator.*

In Apemama, the Stevensons named their living complex "Equator Town," after their ship. Louis and Lloyd wrote The Wrecker *here.*

Their supplies dwindled to salt beef, pork, and wild chickens, the only game. Of these Lloyd wrote: "Ah Fu fried them, grilled them, curried them, minced them; made them into game-pies . . . but the same seagull flavor was always there."

They ate coconuts, too, and huge edible roots, like yams, weighing twenty to forty pounds each. As weeks passed, Fanny began to harvest vegetables from her garden. The shallots, Louis said, "were served out a leaf at a time and welcomed and relished like peaches."

Finally the ship returned, restocked for a crossing to Samoa. On their last evening in Apemama, the king confided in Lloyd: "I very sorry you go . . . Miss Stlevens he good man, woman he good man, boy he good man, all good man. Women he smart all the same man. . . . You no see king cry before. King all the same man: feel bad, he cry. I very sorry."

The next morning Tembinok', dressed in a naval uniform, presented Louis with three mats made of plaited fiber, heavy and strong. Mats, worn as body armor, were precious family heirlooms in the South Pacific, like coats-of-arms. These had belonged to the king's father, uncle, and grandfather.

Fanny is carried ashore at Apang in the Gilbert Islands. Louis wrote of her: "Teacher, tender, comrade wife/A fellow-farer true through life."

THIRTEEN

To the Line Islands: The Cruise of the *Janet Nicholl*

1889–1890

"Come up and see Samoa!" Fanny shouted on December 7, 1889, to Louis, below deck. The *Equator* had reached the island of Upolu, fifty-five miles long, eleven miles wide, largest of the group of fourteen islands known as Samoa, or the Navigator Islands.

The air smelled like "a blend of ylang-ylang blossoms, wood-smoke, and copra" as Upolu took shape before them, with "thickly wooded, lettuce-green hills piled up against a blue sky. Along the beach, fringed with cocoa-nut palms, a row of small shops faced the sea, half hidden by the foliage of trees and shrubs. Lying on the reef and towering out of the water . . . were the hulks of three men-of-war, tragic reminders of the great hurricane that had cost so many lives."

Strolling barefoot down the beach at Apia, Louis wore a white yachting cap, white, loose-fitting clothes, and a red sash.

Apia harbor, Samoa. Louis said Apia was a town full of "grog-shops, its apparently unemployed hangers-on, its merchants of all degrees of respectability and the reverse."

Lloyd, tall and blond, with gold earrings and blue glasses, carried a ukulele. Fanny, in *hokalu* and a broad straw hat, held her guitar. Joe Strong, who usually wore a flowered *lava-lava* (a sarong at the waist) and carried his pet white cockatiel on his shoulder, was with them. Ah Fu's presence added to their exotic look. A missionary who saw them arriving took them for broken-down entertainers.

They stayed with an American trader, Joe Strong's friend

Harry Moors, and Mrs. Moors, a Samoan. Harry was one of three hundred whites and half-castes in Apia, a rough town known as the hell-hole of the Pacific.

Upolu, however, was a paradise. Louis described its "great German [copra] plantations with their countless regular avenues of palms. The island has beautiful rivers . . . with pleasant pools and waterfalls and overhanging verdure, and often a great volume of sound, so that once I thought I was passing near a mill, but it was only the voice of the river."

Through an interpreter, Louis gave a speech at a missionary college. There the Reverend J. E. Newell introduced him as *Tusitala,* the writer of tales, from *tusi,* to write, and *tala,* a story or stories. The nickname stuck, and gained wide recognition around the world.

Samoa pleased Louis: the weather was delightful, he felt healthy there, and boats stopped frequently in Apia, bringing mail and supplies. Soon he decided to buy a "tropical plantation" on Upolu, where he could write and Fanny could farm. This investment would provide for his family, Louis thought, even after his death.

Harry Moors found the site on a mountain, three miles above Apia. Louis wrote to Charles Baxter, "I have bought 314½ acres of beautiful land in the bush behind Apia . . . We range from 600 to 1,500 feet [above sea level], have five streams, waterfalls, precipices, profound ravines, rich tablelands, fifty head of cattle on the ground (if any one could catch them), a great view of forest, sea, mountains, the warships in the haven, really a noble place."

Paying four hundred pounds for the land, Louis named it Vailima, or "the Five Rivers." It included a deserted banana grove and huge banyan trees—home to flying foxes, large fruit-eating bats.

Joe Strong, claiming to have a serious heart condition, left the others to join his wife and son in Australia. The trip had not improved him; he still drank and took opium, and in Sydney he spent the money that Louis sent Belle.

Leaving Harry Moors to build them a house in Samoa, Louis, Fanny, and Lloyd sailed for Sydney, Australia. On arrival, they sent for Belle to come to the Victoria Hotel.

In the lobby, Belle said, "I saw Louis dart out of the 'lift' and walk toward the desk ... boiling with rage." Louis, dressed in a wrinkled, old suit, complained that he had been given a room, not a suite, as requested, and that the clerk had failed to send up his luggage.

Belle wrote of the luggage: "Never, I am sure, had such an amazing array been seen on that polished floor; two or three cedar-wood chests tied with rope, several Tukalau buckets which are made of sections of a tree trunk ... bulging palm leaf baskets, rolls of native *tapa* cloth, fine mats, and an assortment of cocoanut shells and calabashes tied up in fish netting. Those things were not extraordinary to Louis. They were a gentleman's luggage and he was indignant that they had not been sent to his rooms."

At Belle's suggestion, the Stevensons moved to the Oxford Hotel, where they were well treated. Next morning, when Louis's name "blazed across the front page of every newspaper," the clerk and manager of the Victoria Hotel came to the Oxford to apologize. Though they begged Louis to return, he refused, and he enjoyed the fact that the Victoria had to forward baskets of letters to him each day.

Catching cold in Sydney, Louis coughed and hemorrhaged, becoming, he said, "a blooming prisoner ... in my bedroom." He would not survive, the doctor told Fanny, unless she took him north to a warmer climate. But because of a sailors' strike, no ships were sailing. Fanny haunted the wharves, begging anyone who would listen to help her.

Finally she found the *Janet Nicholl,* a combination sail-boat and steamboat, six hundred tons, with an all black crew, unaffected by strikes among white sailors. The *Janet Nicholl's* captain agreed to take Fanny, Louis, and Lloyd on the ship's trading cruise to the Line Islands. Ah Fu had returned to China; they never saw him again.

Fanny and Louis on the SS Janet Nicholl. *A combination sailboat and steamboat, the ship amazed islanders when it sailed against the wind.*

On April 11, 1890, Louis was carried to the ship, "laid out on a board, rolled like a mummy in a blanket," Belle said. He was so ill she feared she would never see him again. But his health improved quickly on his third long cruise through the South Seas.

Their first stop was Auckland, New Zealand. As the ship sailed from Auckland Harbor, Lloyd's cabin exploded, catching the *Janet Nicholl* on fire. Puffing and popping, the flames burned red, blue and green. Rushing to help, Louis puzzled over the bright colors.

Lloyd's roommate had bought fireworks in Auckland, and they had ignited by spontaneous combustion. Fighting thick smoke and pungent fumes, Louis reported: "We got the hose down in time and saved the ship, but Lloyd lost most of his clothes and a great part of our photographs was destroyed. Fanny saw the native sailors tossing overboard a blazing trunk; she stopped them in time, and behold, it contained my manuscripts."

When the ship stopped for one day in Samoa, Louis and Fanny rode horseback to Vailima. The road, shaded by palms and banana trees, ended at the Samoan village of Tanugamanono. From there Harry Moors had constructed a bridle path, a rocky trail through jungle so thick it seemed like a green tunnel.

In a clearing on the mountain stood their new house, painted green on the outside, with a red iron roof. After a quick look around its four rooms, they rode back down to the harbor to continue their trip. Fanny wrote, "at about four we steamed out. Our little house in the bush was visible to the naked eye from the deck of the steamer."

"Natives have said," she also wrote, "that the first sight of white people is dreadful, as they look like corpses walking." But wherever the *Janet Nicholl* stopped in the Line Islands, Louis and his family were welcomed by island dignitaries. They were entertained with dancing, speeches, and the best meals available, and presented necklaces of shark's or human's teeth.

In return the Stevensons gave flowered calico, tobacco, oranges, biscuits [cookies], jam, gold rings, and Fanny's wreaths of artificial flowers. She wore wreaths on her hats and rings on her fingers to take off and give away.

Islanders visited the ship at each stop. Fanny told how "Louis was dictating to Lloyd, who used his typewriter. All the air and most of the light was cut off from them by heads at the port-holes. I watched the faces and saw one intelligent old man explaining to the others that Lloyd was playing an accompaniment to Louis' singing."

In mid-June 1890, Louis received a tearful reception from his friend King Tembinok'. Following a devastating outbreak of measles in Apemama, Tembinok' looked ill, and much older. Fanny gave him a special flag she had ordered for him in Sydney. Bearing his personal symbol, a shark, it was tri-colored, to represent his three islands.

By August 1890, they were back in Australia. Lloyd sailed for England, to sell Skerryvore and Heriot Row, and to bring Maggie and the family furniture back to Vailima.

As usual Louis got sick in Sydney. He wrote to his friend, the author Henry James, "I do not think I shall come to England more than once and then it'll be to die. Health I enjoy in the tropics; even here, which they call sub- or semi-tropical, I come only to catch cold. . . . The thermometer was nearly down to 50 the other day—no temperature for me, Mr. James: how should I do in England?"

In September, Louis and Fanny sailed for Samoa, their new home.

Pineapple Cottage, the first house at Vailima. There Louis heard only the soothing beat of the surf, "the occasional note of a bird, a cry from the boys at work, or the crash of a falling tree."

FOURTEEN

The Clan of Tusitala

1890–1893

Sailing into Apia Harbor for the third time felt pleasantly familiar. "Breaths of the land breeze began to come out to us," said Fanny, "intoxicating with the odours of the earth, of growing trees, sweet flowers and fruits, and dominating all, the clean, wholesome smell of breadfruit baking in hot stones."

Their little cottage provided temporary shelter until a larger house could be built. Soon after moving in, Louis wrote, "The day has just wound up with a shower . . . and how the birds and the frogs are rattling, and piping, and hailing from the woods! . . . Here the showers only patter on the iron roof, and sometimes roar; and within, the lamp burns steady on the tafa-covered walls." When they went out at night, Louis left a lamp burning so he could see his home through the trees as he returned.

The Stevensons bought saddle horses, who promptly ate the roof off their new stable. Apia was three miles down the mountain. Whoever went to town brought back the latest news, and bread and meat if their budget allowed.

Though they fished and hunted birds, food was scarce; on December 29, 1890, Louis wrote, "we have *often* almost nothing to eat . . . my wife and I have dined on one avocado pear."

But the volcanic soil was rich, and Fanny was a good farmer. Louis helped her clear the land, enjoying outdoor work so much that he had to force himself to write. Within two years, they had asparagus, string beans, breadfruit, cacao, chirmoyas, coconuts, eggplants, guavas, lemons, mangoes, onions, oranges, pandanus, parsley, bell peppers, pineapples, sweet potatoes, pumpkins, and tomatoes. Louis prided himself on salads he made from Fanny's garden.

On the front lawn, they laid out two tennis courts. A stream just below the house "plunged over a barrier of rock with a fall of about twelve feet into a delightful pool, just deep enough for bathing."

Historian Henry Adams, who had never met Louis, visited the famous author when he came to Samoa in 1890. He found Louis dressed in "dirty striped pajamas, the baggy legs tucked into coarse woollen stockings, one of which was bright brown in color, the other a purplish dark tone." Fanny, he said, wore "the usual missionary nightgown which was no cleaner than her husband's shirt and drawers, but she omitted the stockings."

"Though I could not forget the dirt and discomfort," Adams continued, "I found Stevenson extremely entertaining. . . . he cannot be quiet, but sits down, jumps up, darts off and flies back . . . looking like an insane stork."

In 1890, Louis's story "The Bottle Imp" was published in the Samoan language in a missionary magazine. Its hero buys a magic bottle with an imp who can make wishes come true. Louis complained later to the translator, "I sometimes almost wish I had not agreed to the printing of *The Bottle Imp* in your paper, for I get such a lot of Samoan visitors who stay a long time, keeping me from my work, and when I am obliged to excuse myself they shyly ask if they might just have a peep at the Imp himself before they go away."

Samoans had difficulty understanding how Louis made his living. To them, he was a chief whose power, like that of all chiefs, came from sorcery and possessions. His wife, considered a possession, seemed magical with her piercing look, forceful manner, foreign plants, and bad-tasting medicines.

Chiefs had special ceremonial mats; Louis's was given to

The family at Vailima. From left to right, back row: *Joe Strong* (with his cockatiel), *Maggie* (sitting), *Lloyd, Louis, Fanny. Belle is in front of Fanny with her son Austin.*

him by a neighboring chief of high standing. When the chiefs called at Vailima, Louis stopped writing to hold *kava*—a ceremony drinking juice made from the root of a pepper plant—and to give speeches on the veranda.

Studying island manners carefully, he tried to follow *fa'a Samoa*—the Samoan way. Thus he did not ask people their names—this was considered rude—and did not discuss pay with his workers. When a servant made a tasty omelette, he praised the man correctly, saying, "Great is your wisdom."

By March 1891, the first phase of the new house was complete. It had waxed floors and the only fireplace in Samoa. Maggie, back from Scotland, paid for a bathhouse.

Lloyd, Fanny, and Louis in the great hall. Vailima was filled with mahogany furniture, Turkish carpets, silver, china, portraits, mirrors, and hundreds of books from Heriot Row and Skerryvore. After going barefoot all day, the family dressed for dinner.

In May 1891, the Strongs arrived at Vailima and moved into the small, original house. When Joe was caught robbing the storeroom and cellars, Belle divorced him. He lived for a time in Apia, then returned to the United States. Belle and Austin became part of Louis's immediate family.

Austin, who was ten in 1891, liked to ride horses and to play the old war game from Davos with Louis and twenty-three-year-old Lloyd. Sometimes Austin attended boarding school, but when at Vailima he studied with Louis and Maggie, reciting poems with a Scottish accent.

Lloyd, who spoke Samoan fluently, was business administrator at Vailima; Fanny supervised the farming. Belle ran the household and helped Louis with his writing.

Servants were hard to find and, until Belle came, hard for the demanding Fanny to keep. Six worked in the house, including one man who starched and fluted Maggie's crisp widow's caps and proudly wore the hats she discarded. Outside, six to thirty workers cared for crops and animals. Male servants brought their families to live at Vailima.

In the Samoan way, Louis and Fanny considered their workers a family clan. On special occasions, the staff wore Scottish tartans, or plaids. At Vailima these were fashioned into the Samoan *lava-lava,* a wraparound piece of fabric worn at the waist by men, under the arms by women.

As head of the family, Louis held councils to punish wrong-doers and led prayer services. At the sound of the *pu,* or conch shell, the clan gathered in the evenings by lamplight, praying and singing in English and Samoan. Louis wrote the *Vailima Prayers,* filling them with ethical values he considered Samoans to need: truthfulness, charity, and industry.

Lloyd sat by Louis "with the Samoan Bible before me, ready to follow him with a chapter in the native language, the rest of the family about us, and in front the long row of half-naked Samoans, with their proud, free air and glistening bodies. We were the *Sa Tusitala,* the clan of Stevenson, and this was the daily enunciation of our solidarity."

Nicknames were a mark of affection for Samoans. Louis joked that *Tusitala* stood for Chief White Information, although usually it was translated as Teller of Tales. Fanny was *Tamaitai,* or Madame; *Aolele,* Beautiful as a flying cloud; and sometimes *O le Fafine Mamana o i le Mauga,* the Witch Woman of the Mountain. Maggie became *Tamaitai Metua,* the old lady. Lloyd was *Loia;* Austin was *Ostini;* and Belle became *Teuila,* Adorner of the Ugly, because she tucked flowers in Samoan girls' hair.

Around the world, Louis's readers were fascinated by the idea that he now lived with "savages." His friend the author Edmund Gosse wrote: "Since Byron was in Greece, nothing has appealed to the ordinary literary man so much as that you should be living in the South Seas."

To support the household, Louis wrote constantly: novels, stories, essays, a journal, and hundreds of letters. Magazine subscriptions kept him aware of new books, which he ordered in English and French.

Rising at dawn to coffee or chocolate and a biscuit, he worked a while, then ate a real breakfast. Dictation to Belle was followed by a swim, lunch, and music—Louis on the flageolet, Lloyd on banjo, Belle on piano—then more writing or a ride into town. Before dinner Louis bathed, changed, and made a cocktail. In the evening, he read the day's work aloud or played cards, and drank a nightcap of whiskey and water. It was a productive schedule; in four years in Samoa, he wrote 700,000 words of printed copy.

This happy life was disrupted often in 1892 and 1893,

Playing cards, probably whist, from left to right: Belle, Louis, Lloyd, Fanny, Maggie

when Fanny suffered from a kidney disease and mental illness. Sometimes she lost her ability to speak. Often she stopped eating. Occasionally she hallucinated, became violent, and tried to run away; then she had to be restrained for her own protection. "Heartbreaking," Louis called his anxiety over her.

At this time, Belle, who always resembled Fanny closely, looked the way Fanny had looked when Louis had met them in France. When Fanny, who had grown stout and gray-haired, felt well enough to worry, she was jealous of her daughter.

In August 1892, Graham Balfour, Louis's cousin, arrived at Vailima. A scholarly young man, Balfour noted his hosts' bare feet and appeared shoeless the second day. Louis said, "Why, he's the same sort of fool that we are!" Belle fell in love with him.

In January 1893, the second phase of the large house was done, paid for by Louis's and Lloyd's novel *The Wrecker.* Downstairs was a great hall, fifty by thirty-five feet, lined with varnished redwood. It held one hundred people for dancing. Upstairs were five bedrooms and a library. The porch, called

Fanny and Louis in Vailima's large hall, paneled with redwood imported from California. "We call these our marble halls," said Lloyd, "because they cost so much."

a veranda, offered a fine view of ships entering Apia harbor. Vailima had an excellent wine cellar and a kitchen in a separate building.

From Heriot Row and Skerryvore, Lloyd had brought furniture, portraits, mirrors, books, linens, silver, and a cottage piano. When company came for dinner, braziers burning under the table in the great hall kept mosquitos away. On important occasions, the clan dressed—staff in blazers and clan *lava-lavas,* Fanny in gray silk or black velvet and lace, and Louis in a starched white jacket, pleated white silk shirt, black dress trousers, and pumps on his narrow feet.

After dinner they sang and, to the tune of the piano, danced Scotch and Irish reels and jigs. One guest reported, "Then arose Tusitala and, placing Teuila (Mrs. Strong) opposite to him, danced on the polished floor with a vigor seldom matched and a delight splendid to see."

Louis's family celebrated all holidays—British, American, and Samoan—entertaining famous visitors and ordinary people with equal enthusiasm. Each year on Louis's birthday, chiefs and their families arrived early at Vailima with presents of turtles, kava root, fans, model canoes, rings, live pigs, rolls of tapa cloth, and fine mats.

Sometimes the guests at Vailima were missionaries. Louis kept an open mind on this subject, writing to a friend who was thinking of entering mission work, "it is a useful and honourable career.... Forget wholly and for ever all small pruderies and remember that *you cannot change ancestral feelings of right and wrong without what is practically soul-murder."*

Louis dictates to his stepdaughter Belle. She "runs me like a baby in a perambulator," he said.

FIFTEEN

War Is Declared

1892–1894

*L*etters took at least two weeks to reach Apia from San Francisco, a month from Liverpool, England. At Vailima, Belle said, "the monthly mail brought up the mountain trail on a pack-saddle was overflowing with requests for [Louis's] autograph, books from young authors begging for a word of approval from 'the Master,' and many letters from the brilliant and successful writers of the day, French, American, and English, praising his latest work and hailing him generously as the greatest of them all."

Samoa's location, on the trade routes, and its copra wealth, needed for coconut oil, made it valuable to Western conquerors. When Louis arrived, Samoa was ruled by three countries: Britain used it as a naval base, the United States sent traders, and Germany, strongest of the three, controlled the copra plantations. The three nations fought for power, backing different island chiefs. Louis described "three consuls, all at loggerheads with one another . . . three different sets of missionaries, not upon the best of terms . . . The native population, very genteel, very songful, very agreeable, very good-looking, [was] chronically spoiling for a fight."

He was horrified by the way the Germans treated their laborers, about eight hundred "blackbirded," or semi-kidnapped Melanesians, almost slaves. One runaway sought refuge at Vailima. When Louis saw his back covered with welts from beatings, he paid for the man's time, adding him to the clan of *Tusitala*.

Outraged, Louis complained to the London *Times* about what the Western powers, especially Germany, were doing to Samoa. In 1892 his protests were published as a book, *A Footnote to History.*

To silence Louis, the British consul threatened to deport him. Louis wrote then of his new house: "It will be a fine legacy to the Imperial German Majesty's protectorate and doubtless the Governor will take it for his country house." But the British backed down, afraid to deport the famous author, and to Louis's surprise, the German government responded to his criticism by dismissing two of their most obnoxious officials.

In 1892, Louis wrote to author Mark Twain, "I wish you could see my 'simple and sunny heaven' now; war has broken out, 'they' have been long in making it, 'they' have worked hard, and here it is—with its concomitants of blackened faces, severed heads and men dying in hospital. . . . the government troops have started a horrid novelty: taking women's heads. . . . all my friends . . . are in the rebellion."

Like most Samoans, Louis supported a chief named Mataafa, from a village west of Apia. Defying German orders, Louis visited that "beautiful, sweet old fellow." Mataafa responded by according Louis "royal" *kava,* the highest honor of Samoan etiquette, with great political impact.

In the summer of 1893, Louis wrote to a friend, "The hills and my house at less than (boom) a minute's interval quake with thunder; and though I cannot hear that part of it, shells are falling thick into the fort of Lotoanuu (boom).... The thought of the poor devils [Mataafa's troops] in the fort (boom) with their bits of rifles [is] far from pleasant."

Vailima as completed, with the Stevenson family at right. After Louis died, the German governor took Vailima for his residence. It has since become the Robert Louis Stevenson Museum.

Horrified at the violence, Louis arranged for use of the Apia public hall as a hospital and assisted at bloody operations on wounded Mataafa partisans. In the end, Mataafa and the major chiefs who supported him were exiled to the German-controlled Marshall Islands; minor chiefs were jailed in Apia.

Louis told reporters, "I can see but one way out—to follow the demand of the Samoan people that the [treaty] be rescinded, while the three Powers withdraw absolutely, and the natives be let alone, and allowed to govern the islands as they choose."

On November 15, 1893, Louis hired a carriage and drove Fanny, Belle, and Lloyd to the jail in Apia. In a brave public

Samoan chiefs, shown here, built a road to Vailima. The sign read: "We bear in mind the surpassing kindness of Mr. R. L. Stevenson and his loving care during our tribulations while in prison."

show of support, they delivered tobacco and *kava* to the imprisoned chiefs. In December the chiefs hosted an elaborate dinner inside the jail for Louis and his family.

After September 1894, the chiefs were gradually released. To honor Louis, they built a road to Vailima, the *ala Loto Alofa,* or the "Road of the Loving Heart."

Louis, who had been studying Samoan, delivered an impassioned speech in Samoan when the road was opened. He wrote to Cummy:

> MY DEAR CUMMY—So I hear you are ailing? Think shame to yourself! So you think there is nothing better to be done with time than that? . . . We are all pretty well. . . . Lloyd has a gymnastic machine, and practises upon it every morning for an hour: he is beginning to be a kind of young Samson. Austin grows fat and brown, and gets on not so ill with his lessons and my mother is in great price. . . . We have had a very interesting business here. I helped the chiefs who were in prison; and when they were set free, what should they do but offer to make a part of my road for me out of gratitude? Well, I was ashamed to refuse, and the trumps dug my road for me, and put up this inscription on a board:—
> *"Considering the great love of His Excellency Tusitala in his loving care of us in our tribulation in the prison, we have made this great gift; it shall never be muddy, it shall go on for ever his road that we have dug!"* . . . . Weel, guid-bye to ye and joy be wi' ye! I hae nae time to say mair.

The novels Louis wrote at Vailima alternated between Scotland and the South Seas. *The Beach of Falesa* tells of a white trader who marries a noble island girl. Louis called this book "the first realistic South Sea story; I mean with real South Sea characters and details of life. Everybody else who has tried that I have seen, got carried away by the romance and ended in a kind of sugar candy epic. . . . Now I have got the smell, and the look of the thing a good deal."

With Lloyd, Louis collaborated on *The Ebb Tide,* a tale of beachcombers and a drunken voyage. "There are only four characters, to be sure," said Louis, "but they are really such a troop of swine! And their behaviour is really so deeply beneath any possible standard, that on a retrospect I wonder I have been able to endure them myself until the yarn was finished."

His Scottish novels of this time included *The Weir of Hermiston, St. Ives,* a love story set in the Pentland Hills at Swanston, and *Catriona,* a sequel to *Kidnapped.* Louis wrote to author J. M. Barrie: "the continuation of *Kidnapped* is under way. I have not yet got to Alan, but David seems to have a kick or two in his shanks." Of *The Weir of Hermiston,* Louis said, "It is pretty Scotch....The heroine is seduced by one man, and finally disappears with the other man who shot him."

Louis wrote to Colvin about Scotland: "Singular that I should fulfil the Scots destiny... and live a voluntary exile, and have my head filled with the blessed, beastly place all the time!" The letters he wrote and received helped him feel close to people and places he had not seen for years. In 1894, Louis learned that William Henley's five-year-old daughter had died. Breaking his long silence, he wrote a warm letter to his old friend.

On November 29, 1894, the clan celebrated Thanksgiving. After dinner, Belle reported, Louis thanked Fanny, to whom, he said, he owed, "not only his happiest years . . . but, through her tender care, his very life as well. He was thankful that his mother was with him; she, who for love of him, had forsaken all other ties and the habit of years to cruise in wild seas to strange islands, and was now safe and near under his

Fanny, Louis, Belle, and Maggie in her widow's cap pose for a formal photograph in 1893.

roof. He was thankful for the two he looked on as son and daughter, who graced his home. Smiling at Austin, he said: 'Vailima is blessed—there's a child in the house.'"

Louis was especially happy that Fanny's health had improved. Of her, he wrote: "She runs the show. Infinitely little, extraordinary wig of gray curls, handsome waxen face like Napoleon's, insane black eyes, boy's hands, tiny bare feet, a cigarette, wild blue native dress, usually spotted with garden mould. . . . Doctors everybody, will doctor you, cannot be doctored herself. A violent friend, a brimstone enemy. Is always either loathed or slavishly adored—indifference impossible. . . . Dreams dreams and sees visions."

Louis and Lloyd in 1894. Louis described himself as "exceeding lean, rather ruddy, black eyes, crows-footed, beginning to be grizzled. . . . The Tame Celebrity."

SIXTEEN

Requiem

1894

On December 3, 1894, Fanny had a foreboding: something dreadful was about to happen to someone very close to them. Could it be Graham Balfour, she wondered, traveling through the islands in rickety old boats, or Charles Baxter, who was on his way to Samoa?

At lunch Louis teased her and tried to distract her, but he could not. In the afternoon, he dictated to Belle, then rode to Apia, returning to Vailima for a swim before dinner.

Wearing a velvet jacket, Louis came downstairs at sunset and tried again to console his wife. He described a lecture tour to the United States and played cards with her, but nothing helped. Fetching a good Burgundy from the wine cellar, he offered to make mayonnaise for the dinner salad. Soon he was mixing oil and lime juice on the veranda.

Suddenly he dropped his spoon and put his long, bony hands to his head. "What's that?" he cried. "Oh, what a pain!"

"Do I look strange?" he asked Fanny, falling to his knees.

"No," she lied, rushing forward to catch him. The butler helped her guide him inside to his grandfather's armchair, in the long hall.

Hearing Fanny's cries, Maggie and Belle came at once. Lloyd, swimming in the pool nearby, jumped out and ran to the house. They found Louis unconscious and red-faced, breathing hoarsely, his open eyes unseeing.

Calling his name and fanning him, they put brandy to his lips, but nothing roused him. Servants brought a cot, and Lloyd helped carry his stepfather to the bed. When the women removed Louis's boots, Lloyd protested, for he knew that Louis wanted to die with his boots on.

Then Lloyd rode their fastest horse to Apia, for the doctor. Dr. Funk, a German, jumped on Lloyd's lathered horse and galloped up the mountain. Stealing a horse tied outside a store, Lloyd overtook the doctor and they reached Vailima together.

But medicine could not help Louis. "A blood clot on the brain," Dr. Funk diagnosed. "He is dying."

Louis died quietly at 8:10 P.M., his clan around him, a dozen Samoans seated on the floor.

As the doctor departed, he told Lloyd in a low voice, "You must bury him before three to-morrow." Noting Lloyd's look of horror, Dr. Funk murmured an explanation: bodies had to be buried quickly in the tropics.

"But I was thinking of that path to Vaea," Lloyd said later, "that path I had never made; of [Louis's] wish which I had always thwarted." Louis had told Lloyd that he wanted to be buried at the peak of Mount Vaea, one thousand feet above Vailima through the thickest jungle.

"In desperation," said Lloyd, "I sent out messengers to several of my closest friends—chiefs . . . I needed two hundred men at dawn, and explained the urgency. But [how could we get] the axes, the bush knives, the mattocks, picks, spades, and crowbars?"

As word of Louis's death and Lloyd's great need spread, a shop opened in town to provide tools and mourning clothes for the workers, hundreds of white undershirts and dozens of bolts of black cotton cloth for *lava-lavas*. A missionary volunteered to find a coffin; the family gave him a list of those to be invited to the funeral the next day at two o'clock.

"Late that night," said Lloyd, "we washed his body and dressed it in a soft white-linen shirt and black evening trousers girded with a dark-blue silk sash. A white tie, dark-blue silk socks, and patent leather shoes completed the costume." They left his silver wedding ring on his finger and a pin, the bronze thistle of Scotland, on his lapel. Placing his body on the big table in the center of the great hall, they covered it with the large Union Jack that usually flew over Vailima.

Soon chiefs began arriving, many of the same chiefs who had built Louis's road. They brought bright flowers and valuable old mats which they piled on Louis's body until the flag was covered.

"Samoa ends with you, Tusitala," said one.

Begging Fanny, Maggie, Lloyd, and Belle to go to bed, the Samoans sat with the body all night, chanting prayers in Latin, English, and Samoan.

"Before dawn," said Lloyd, "Vailima began to seethe with men, one little army after another, marching up with its chiefs. . . . All that morning the still air was broken by the crash of trees; the ringing sound of axes, the hoarser thud of mattocks and crowbars pounding on rocks. But the men themselves had been warned to make no sound; there was none of the singing and laughter that was such an inseparable part of concerted work."

At the top of the mountain, workers felled trees to make a room-sized clearing for the grave. Lloyd wrote: "At two o'clock the coffin was brought out by a dozen powerful Samoans, who led the way with it up the mountain. Directly behind were thirty or forty more men, who at intervals changed places with the bearers. It was a point of honor with them all to keep their heavy burden shoulder-high, though how they contrived to do so on that precipitous path was a seeming impossibility. A party of a score or more white people followed, interspersed with chiefs of high rank. Behind these, again, were perhaps two hundred Samoans, all in the white singlets and black lavalavas which had been given them for that day of mourning."

Mourners at the grave on Mt. Vaea. After the funeral, the local chief tapued the use of firearms in the area, so Louis could hear the birds he loved.

In the stifling heat, some guests could not climb all the way to the summit, 1,300 feet above sea level. Nineteen Europeans and sixty Samoans reached the top.

After a short rest, the Reverend W. E. Clarke read the burial service of the Church of England, including a prayer Louis had written and read aloud to his family the day before his death: "We beseech Thee, Lord, to behold us with favour, folk of many families and nations, gathered together in the peace of this roof."

In 1897 a monument was placed over the grave, with two bronze plaques. One is inscribed in Samoan: "The Tomb of Tusitala." It contains Ruth's speech to Naomi, taken from the Samoan Bible: "Whither thou goest I will go; and where thou lodgest, I will lodge: thy people shall be my people, and thy God my God: where thou diest, will I die, and there will I be buried." It is decorated with a thistle, for Scotland, and a hibiscus flower, for Samoa.

On the other plaque, in English, is Louis's most famous poem, "Requiem."

> Under the wide and starry sky,
> Dig the grave and let me lie.
> Glad did I live and gladly die,
> And I laid me down with a will.
>
> This be the verse you grave for me:
> *Here he lies where he longed to be;*
> *Home is the sailor, home from sea,*
> *And the hunter home from the hill.*

Sources

p.8   Robert Louis Stevenson, *A Child's Garden of Verses,* illus. Jessie Willcox Smith (New York: Scribner's, 1905), 9.

p.9   Robert Louis Stevenson, *In the South Seas,* The Biographical Edition of the Works of Robert Louis Stevenson. (New York: Scribner's, 1892), 5.

pp.9–10   Margaret Stevenson, *From Saranac to the Marquesas and Beyond* (New York: Scribner's, 1903), 73.

p.10   RLS, *In the South Seas,* 8.

p.10   *The Letters of Robert Louis Stevenson to His Family and Friends,* ed. Sidney Colvin, 2 vols. (New York: Scribner's, 1899), 2:189.

p.12   J. C. Furnas, *Voyage to Windward: The Life of Robert Louis Stevenson* (New York: William Sloane, 1951), 7.

p.12   Margaret Mackay, *The Violent Friend: The Story of Mrs. Robert Louis Stevenson* (New York: Doubleday, 1968), 37.

p.12   Graham Balfour, *The Life of Robert Louis Stevenson* (New York: Scribner's, 1911), 33.

p.13   Ian Bell, *Dreams of Exile: Robert Louis Stevenson, A Biography* (New York: Scribner's, 1992), 24.

p.13   RLS to Charles Baxter, The Beinecke Rare Book and Manuscript Library, Yale University.

p.14   Bell, *Dreams of Exile,* 32.

p.14   Furnas, *Voyage to Windward,* 18.

p.16   Ibid.

p.17   Robert Louis Stevenson, *Memories and Portraits* (New York: Scribner's, 1906), 101.

p.18   RLS, *A Child's Garden of Verses,* 20.

p.18   Bell, *Dreams of Exile,* 29.

pp.18–19   Balfour, *The Life of Robert Louis Stevenson,* 29.

p.19   Bell, *Dreams of Exile,* 23.

p.22   Ibid., 36.

p.22   Balfour, *The Life of Robert Louis Stevenson,* 52.

p.23   Ibid., 65.

p.23   Bell, *Dreams of Exile,* 7.

pp.23–24   RLS, *Memories and Portraits,* 55–56.

p.24   Balfour, *The Life of Robert Louis Stevenson,* 66.

p.25   Balfour, *The Life of Robert Louis Stevenson,* 64.

p.26   Bell, *Dreams of Exile,* 68.

p.27   Balfour, *The Life of Robert Louis Stevenson,* 68.

p.28   Robert Louis Stevenson, *The Silverado Squatters,* 251.

p.28   RLS, *Memories and Portraits,* 18.

p.29   Balfour, *The Life of Robert Louis Stevenson,* 73.

p.29   Bell, *Dreams of Exile,* 69.

p.29   Balfour, *The Life of Robert Louis Stevenson,* 63.

p.29   Ibid., 86.

p.30   Furnas, *Voyage to Windward,* 55.

p.30   Balfour, *The Life of Robert Louis Stevenson,* 79.

p.30 Rosalie Masson, ed., *I Can Remember Robert Louis Stevenson* (New York: Frederick A. Stokes, 1922), 80.

p.32 *The Letters*, 1:45–46.

p.32 Frank McLynn, *Robert Louis Stevenson: A Biography* (New York: Random House, 1993), 61.

p.32 RLS to Mrs. Sitwell, National Library of Scotland, Edinburgh.

p.32 Bell, *Dreams of Exile*, 71.

p.33 Masson, *I Can Remember*, 110.

p.35 RLS to Mrs. Sitwell, National Library of Scotland.

p.36 Furnas, *Voyage to Windward*, 88.

p.36 RLS to Mrs. Sitwell, National Library of Scotland.

p.36 Ibid.

p.37 *The Letters*, 1:98.

p.37 Ibid., 1:108.

p.37 Masson, *I Can Remember*, 81.

p.38 Robert Louis Stevenson, *An Island Voyage*, 9.

p.38 Ibid., 28.

p.38 Ibid., 70.

pp.38–39 Masson, *I Can Remember*, 218–219.

p.39 *The Letters*, 1:399.

p.41 Lloyd Osbourne, *An Intimate Portrait of RLS* (New York: Scribner's, 1924), 1. Reprinted with the permission of Scribner, a Division of Simon & Schuster.

p.42 Isobel Field, *This Life I've Loved* (New York: Longmans, Green, 1937), 105.

p.44 Bell, *Dreams of Exile*, 113.

p.45 *The Letters*, 1: 148.

p.46 RLS to R. A. M. Stevenson, Beinecke Library.

p.47 Robert Louis Stevenson, *The Amateur Emigrant* (Chicago: Stone & Kimball, 1895), 135.

p.47 Balfour, *The Life of Robert Louis Stevenson*, 145.

p.47 RLS, *The Amateur Emigrant*, 157.

p.48 *The Letters*, 1:166.

p.48 Bell, *Dreams of Exile*, 134.

p.48 Ibid.

p.48 Osbourne, *An Intimate Portrait of RLS*, 14.

p.48 Field, *This Life I've Loved*, 119.

p.48 Osbourne, *An Intimate Portrait of RLS*, 16–17.

p.49 RLS to Charles Baxter, Beinecke Library.

p.49 RLS, *The Silverado Squatters*, 225.

p.50 *The Letters*, 1:186.

p.50 Osbourne, *An Intimate Portrait of RLS*, 21.

p.50 Ibid.

pp.50–51 Ibid, 22.

p.51 Balfour, *The Life of Robert Louis Stevenson*, 156.

p.51 Thomas Stevenson to Sidney Colvin, Beinecke Library.

p.51 *The Letters*, 1:200.

p.51 Masson, *I Can Remember*, 240.

p.52 RLS, *The Silverado Squatters*, 253.

p.52 Ibid., 278.

p.52 Bell, *Dreams of Exile*, 141.

p.52 RLS, *The Silverado Squatters*, 236.

p.53 Ibid., 293.

p.55 Bell, *Dreams of Exile*, 144.

p.55 Ibid.

p.56 E. V. Lucas, *The Colvins and Their Friends* (New York: Scribner's, 1928).

p.56 Mackay, *The Violent Friend*, 133.

p.56 Furnas, *Voyage to Windward*, 185.

p.56 Balfour, *The Life of Robert Louis Stevenson*, 159.

p.57 *The Letters*, 1:215.

p.58 Ibid., 1:257.

p.58 Ibid., 1:257–258.

p.60 Balfour, *The Life of Robert Louis Stevenson*, 166.

p.61 RLS, *A Child's Garden of Verses*, 49.

p.61 RLS to William Henley, National Library of Scotland.

p.61 Osbourne, *An Intimate Portrait of RLS*, 36.

p.62 Masson, *I Can Remember*, 169.

p.63 *The Works of Robert Louis Stevenson*, South Seas Edition, 26 vols. (New York: Scribner's, 1892), 2:121.

p.63 *The Letters*, 1:364–365.

p.64 RLS, *A Child's Garden of Verses*, 8.

p.64 Ibid., 23–24.

p.65 *The Letters*, 1:311.

p.65 Robert Louis Stevenson, *Treasure Island* (New York: Scribner's, 1911), v.

p.66 Osbourne, *An Intimate Portrait of RLS*, 49.

p.66 Balfour, *The Life of Robert Louis Stevenson*, 184.

p.66 Ibid., 178.

p.67 Bell, *Dreams of Exile*, 165.

p.68 Osbourne, *An Intimate Portrait of RLS*, 53.

p.68 Furnas, *Voyage to Windward*, 250.

p.68 Bell, *Dreams of Exile*, 182.

p.69 RLS, *A Child's Garden of Verses*, v.

pp.69–70 Balfour, *The Life of Robert Louis Stevenson*, 37.

p.70 Osbourne, *An Intimate Portrait of RLS*, 63.

p.70 Ibid., 63–64.

pp.70–71 Ibid., 64.

p.71 Ibid., 65.

p.71 Ibid., 62.

p.72 *The Letters*, 1:399.

p.73 Ibid., 2:73

p.73 M. Stevenson, *From Saranac to the Marquesas*, 9.

p.74 *The Letters*, 2:81.

p.75 Furnas, *Voyage to Windward*, 285.

p.75 RLS to Charles Baxter, National Library of Scotland.

p.75 RLS, *A Child's Garden of Verses*, 13.

p.76 Osbourne, *An Intimate Portrait of RLS*, 82.

p.76 Ibid., 79–80.

p.76 *The Letters*, 2:116.

p.76 McLynn, *Robert Louis Stevenson*, 310.

p.77 *The Letters*, 2:173.

p.78 *The Wrecker*, 221.

p.79 Furnas, *Voyage to Windward*, 307.

p.79 M. Stevenson, *From Saranac to the Marquesas*, 68.

p.79 Arthur Johnstone, *Recollections of Robert Louis Stevenson in the Pacific* (London: Chatto & Windus, 1905), 16.

p.80 M. Stevenson, *From Saranac to the Marquesas*, 63, 71.

p.80 Alexandra Lapierre, *Fanny Stevenson: A Romance of Destiny*, trans. Carol Cosman (New York: Carroll & Graf, 1995), 363.

pp.80–81 M. Stevenson, *From Saranac to the Marquesas*, 70.

p.81 Ibid., 76.
p.81 RLS, *In the South Seas,* 9.
p.81 Ibid.
p.81 Ibid., 13–14.
p.82 Ibid., 19.
p.82 Ibid., 89–90.
pp.82–83 Ibid., 56.
p.83 *The Letters,* 2:141.
p.83 M. Stevenson, *From Saranac to the Marquesas,* 81.
pp.83–84 RLS, *In the South Seas,* 16–17.
p.84 Ibid., 60.
p.84 Ibid., 39.
p.85 *The Letters,* 2:148.
p.86 Ibid., 2:150.
p.86 Ibid., 2:152.
p.86 Ibid., 2:141.
p.86 Ibid., 2:144.
p.87 M. Stevenson, *From Saranac to the Marquesas,* 229–230.
p.88 *R. L. S. in the South Seas,* ed. Alanna Knight (Edinburgh: Mainstream Publishing, 1986), 102.
p.89 Field, *This Life I've Loved,* 222.
pp.89–90 M. Stevenson, *From Saranac to the Marquesas,* 258.
p.90 Osbourne, *An Intimate Portrait of RLS,* 90.
p.91 *The Letters,* 2:140.
p.91 Field, *This Life I've Loved,* 156.
p.92 Balfour, *The Life of Robert Louis Stevenson,* 188.
p.93 Ibid., 251.
p.93 Mackay, *The Violent Friend,* 285.
p.95 Bell, *Dreams of Exile,* 237.
p.95 Mackay, *The Violent Friend,* 280.
p.96 RLS to Charles Baxter, Beinecke Library.

p.96 RLS, *In the South Seas,* 277.
p.96 *R. L. S. in the South Seas,* 139.
p.97 RLS, *In the South Seas,* 278.
p.97 Ibid., 284.
p.98 Ibid., 332.
p.98 Ibid., 333.
p.98 Ibid., 265.
pp.98–99 Osbourne, *An Intimate Portrait of RLS,* 103.
p.99 RLS, *In the South Seas,* 368.
p.100 Ibid., 365.
p.101 Osbourne, *An Intimate Portrait of RLS,* 109.
p.101 RLS, *In the South Seas,* 349.
p.101 Balfour, *The Life of Robert Louis Stevenson,* 261.
p.102 RLS, *The Works of Robert Louis Stevenson,* 12.
p.103 Mackay, *The Violent Friend,* 303.
p.103 Field, *This Life I've Loved,* 279.
p.103 Ibid.
p.104 *The Letters,* 2:228.
p.105 Ibid., 2:208.
p.105 Ibid., 2:213.
p.106 Field, *This Life I've Loved,* 266.
p.106 Ibid.
p.106 Bell, *Dreams of Exile,* 267.
p.106 *The Letters,* 2:219.
p.108 Field, *This Life I've Loved,* 273–274.
p.108 *The Letters,* 2:222.
p.108 Fanny Stevenson, *The Cruise of the "Janet Nichol" Among the South Sea Islands* (New York: Scribner's, 1914), 32.
p.108 *R. L. S. in the South Seas,* 176.
p.109 F. Stevenson, *The Cruise of the "Janet Nichol,"* 112.
p.109 *The Letters,* 2:235.
p.110 Balfour, *The Life of Robert Louis Stevenson,* 288.

p.111   F. Stevenson, *The Cruise of the "Janet Nichol,"* 28–29.

p.111   *The Letters,* 2:250–251.

p.112   Ibid., 2:255.

p.112   Balfour, *The Life of Robert Louis Stevenson,* 286.

p.112   Furnas, *Voyage to Windward,* 370.

p.112   Ibid.

pp.112–113   Masson, *I Can Remember,* 315.

p.114   Furnas, *Voyage to Windward,* 387.

pp.115–116   Masson, *I Can Remember,* 309.

p.116   Balfour, *The Life of Robert Louis Stevenson,* 285.

p.118   *The Letters,* 2:372.

p.118   Mackay, *The Violent Friend,* 410.

p.119   Masson, *I Can Remember,* 337.

p.119   *The Letters,* 2:408.

p.120   Mackay, *The Violent Friend,* 426.

p.121   Isobel Field, *Robert Louis Stevenson* (Los Angeles: Warren F. Lewis, 1950), 23.

pp.121–122   *The Letters,* 2:228.

p.122   Forbes Macgregor, *Robert Louis Stevenson* (Great Britain: Jarrold & Sons, 1989), 189.

p.122   Bell, *Dreams of Exile,* 258.

p.122   Furnas, *Voyage to Windward,* 399.

p.123   *The Letters,* 2:359.

p.124   Furnas, *Voyage to Windward,* 403.

p.124   Ibid., 406.

p.125   *The Letters,* 2:431–432.

pp.125–126   *The Works of Robert Louis Stevenson,* South Seas Edition, 2:121.

p.126   *The Letters,* 2:353.

p.126   Ibid., 2:296.

p.126   Ibid., 2:327.

p.126   *R. L. S. in the South Seas,* 25.

pp.126–127   Field, *This Life I've Loved,* 341–342.

p.127   Mackay, *The Violent Friend,* 425.

p.128   Furnas, *Voyage to Windward,* 410–411.

p.129   Balfour, *The Life of Robert Louis Stevenson,* 330–331.

p.129   Furnas, *Voyage to Windward,* 431.

p.129   Balfour, *The Life of Robert Louis Stevenson,* 331.

p.130   Furnas, *Voyage to Windward,* 431.

p.130   Osbourne, *An Intimate Portrait of RLS,* 145.

p.130   Ibid.

p.130   Ibid.

pp.130–131   Ibid., 146.

p.131   Ibid., 147.

p.131   Osbourne, *An Intimate Portrait of RLS,* 151.

p.131   Ibid., 149–150.

p.132   Ibid., 152–153.

p.133   Balfour, *The Life of Robert Louis Stevenson,* 333–334.

p.133   Ruth 1:16–17.

p.133   RLS, *The Works of Robert Louis Stevenson,* 26.

Selected Bibliography

Writings of Robert Louis Stevenson

The Amateur Emigrant. 1895.

The Black Arrow. 1888.

Catriona. 1893.

A Child's Garden of Verses. 1885.

Edinburgh: Picturesque Notes. Ill. by T. Hamilton Crawford. London: Seeley and Co., 1896.

A Footnote to History: Eight Years of Troubles in Samoa. New York: Scribner's, 1895.

In the South Seas. The Biographical Edition of the Works of Robert Louis Stevenson. New York: Scribner's, 1892.

An Inland Voyage. 1878.

Kidnapped. 1886.

The Letters of Robert Louis Stevenson to His Family and Friends. 2 vols. Edited by Sidney Colvin. New York: Scribner's, 1899.

The Master of Ballantrae. 1889.

Memories and Portraits. New York: Scribner's, 1906.

New Arabian Nights. 1882.

Prince Otto. 1885.

R. L. S. in the South Seas. Edited by Alanna Knight. Edinburgh: Mainstream Publishing, 1986.

St. Ives: The Adventures of a French Prisoner in England. 1990.

The Silverado Squatters. 1883.

The Strange Case of Dr. Jekyll and Mr. Hyde. 1886.

Travels with a Donkey in the Cévennes. 1879.

Treasure Island. 1883.

"Virginibus Puerisque" and Other Papers. New York: Current Literature Publishing, 1906.

The Weir of Hermiston. 1894.

The Works of Robert Louis Stevenson. South Seas Edition. 26 vols. New York: Scribner's, 1892.

The Wrecker. With Lloyd Osbourne. 1892.

The Wrong Box. With Lloyd Osbourne. 1894.

Other Sources

Balfour, Graham. *The Life of Robert Louis Stevenson.* New York: Scribner's, 1911.

Bell, Ian. *Dreams of Exile: Robert Louis Stevenson, A Biography.* New York: Henry Holt, 1992.

Cohen, Edward H. *The Henley-Stevenson Quarrel.* Gainesville: University Presses of Florida, 1974.

Daiches, David. *Robert Louis Stevenson.* Norfolk, CT: New Directions, 1947.

Field, Isobel. *Robert Louis Stevenson.* Los Angeles: Warren F. Lewis, 1950.

———. *This Life I've Loved.* New York: Longmans, Green, 1937.

Furnas, J. C. *Voyage to Windward: The Life of Robert Louis Stevenson.* New York: William Sloane, 1951.

Geddie, John. *The Home Country of R. L. Stevenson: Being the Valley of the Water of Leith from Source to Sea.* Edinburgh: W. H. White, 1898.

Gherman, Beverly. *Robert Louis Stevenson: Teller of Tales.* New York: Atheneum, 1996.

Grover, Eulalie Osgood. *Robert Louis Stevenson: Teller of Tales.* New York: Dodd, Mead, 1942.

Hill, Robin A. *R. L. S., Francophile: Robert Louis Stevenson in France.* Edinburgh, 1993.

Kay, Robert F. *Tahiti & French Polynesia.* 3rd ed. Oakland, CA: Lonely Planet, 1992.

Lapierre, Alexandra. *Fanny Stevenson: A Romance of Destiny.* Translated by Carol Cosman. New York: Carroll & Graf, 1995.

Lucas, E. V. *The Colvins and Their Friends.* New York: Scribner's, 1928.

Mackay, Margaret. *The Violent Friend: The Story of Mrs. Robert Louis Stevenson.* New York: Doubleday, 1968.

Masson, Rosaline, ed. *I Can Remember Robert Louis Stevenson.* New York: Frederick A. Stokes, 1922.

McLaren, Moray. *Stevenson and Edinburgh: A Centenary Study.* London: Chapman & Hall, 1950.

McLynn, Frank. *Robert Louis Stevenson: A Biography.* New York: Random House, 1993.

Murphy, Jim. *Across America on an Emigrant Train.* New York: Clarion, 1993.

Osbourne, Lloyd. *An Intimate Portrait of RLS.* New York: Scribner's, 1924.

Sanchez, Nellie Van de Grift. *The Life of Mrs. Robert Louis Stevenson.* New York: Scribner's, 1920.

Sarolea, Charles. *Robert Louis Stevenson and France.* Edinburgh: The Robert Louis Stevenson Foundation, 1976.

Stanley, David. *South Pacific Handbook.* 5th ed. Chico, CA: Moon Publications, 1993.

———. *Tahiti-Polynesia Handbook.* Chico, CA: Moon Publications, 1992.

Stevenson, Fanny. *The Cruise of the "Janet Nichol" Among the South Sea Islands: A Diary by Mrs. Robert Louis Stevenson.* New York: Scribner's, 1914.

———. *Our Samoan Adventure.* New York: Harper & Brothers, 1955.

Stevenson, Margaret. *From Saranac to the Marquesas and Beyond.* New York: Charles Scribner's Sons, 1903.

Swaney, Deanna. *Samoa: Western & American Samoa.* 2nd ed. Oakland, CA: Lonely Planet, 1994.

Willard, Nancy. *The Voyage of the Ludgate Hill: Travels with Robert Louis Stevenson.* Ill. by Alice and Martin Provensen. San Diego: Harcourt Brace Jovanovich, 1987.

Index

Photo Acknowledgments

The photographs and illustrations are reproduced with the permission of:
Archive Photos, pp. 1, 62, 118; The Writers' Museum, Edinburgh, pp. 2, 8, 11,
13, 16, 19, 20, 25, 31, 34, 44, 54, 56, 60, 67, 72, 74, 78, 83, 85, 91, 94, 96, 99, 100,
102, 104, 107, 110, 113, 114, 120, 123, 127, 128, 132; The Trustees of the
National Library of Scotland, pp. 15, 28, 77, 92; Corbis-Bettmann, pp. 26, 88,
117; Silverado Museum, pp. 39, 53; The City of Edinburgh Museums, p. 40;
UPI/Corbis-Bettmann, p. 46; The Letters of Robert Louis Stevenson, p. 49;
N. C. Wyeth, Attack on the Block House, Collection of the Brandywine River
Museum, Gift of Mr. and Mrs. Bayard Sharp, p. 59; Jessie Willcox Smith, A
Child's Garden of Verses, p. 64; N. C. Wyeth, The Wreck of the "Covenant,"
1913, Collection of the Brandywine River Museum, Gift of Mrs. Russell G.
Colt, p. 69; Archive Photos/Popperfoto, p. 124.

Front cover portrait: The Stevenson House Collection, Monterey State
Historic Park, California Department of Parks and Recreation. Front cover
illustration: N. C. Wyeth, The Hostage, 1911, Collection of the Brandywine
River Museum, Bequest of Mrs. Gertrude Haskell Britton. Back cover
photograph: © The Writers' Museum, Edinburgh.